1. Introduction

The Federal Housing Administration (FHA) administers mortgage insurance programs that provide guarantees for first-time home buyers and other borrowers who might otherwise find it difficult to obtain a mortgage. Under the terms of FHA's insurance, FHA agrees to reimburse the mortgage lender for the unpaid balance of the loan and any accrued interest if the borrower defaults on the scheduled mortgage payments. In return, FHA charges the borrower fees. In the event of default and foreclosure, FHA takes possession of the mortgaged property and sells it to cover a portion of its losses. From 2008 through 2013, FHA insured over 20 percent of the mortgages made to purchasers of single family homes each year, which is significantly higher than in prior years (see Figure 1.1). That increase stems largely from the reduced availability of private mortgages in the wake of the financial crisis.

In accordance with its role of extending credit to home buyers who would have difficulty obtaining alternative sources of mortgage financing, FHA's loan requirements are generally less stringent than those available elsewhere in the market. FHA currently requires a minimum down payment of 3.5 percent of the property value, lower than what is required by most other guarantors. FHA borrowers have, historically, had lower credit scores than other borrowers (see, for instance, Pennington-Cross and Nichols 2000). Because of the elevated risk profile of those borrowers, FHA loans have generally defaulted at higher rates than the national average (see Figure 1.2). However, credit scores of new FHA borrowers have improved substantially since 2009 (see, for instance, Department of Housing and Urban Development various years). That shift has occurred because FHA has tightened its eligibility standards and because alternative sources of financing for low down payment loans have become scarcer, even for borrowers with high credit scores.

FHA is required to set fees for its insurance so that the discounted value (using Treasury rates for discounting) of projected fee income is greater than that of projected losses from defaults. The initial surplus (i.e., the negative subsidy amount) from each year's newly-made loan guarantees is added to the capital reserve of the Mutual Mortgage Insurance Fund (MMIF), and the MMIF balance is adjusted on an annual basis for changes in realized and estimated net surpluses associated with past cohorts of loans as projected by the Office of Management and Budget (OMB). The capital reserve serves primarily as a means of reconciling the accrual method of accounting for mortgage guarantees in the budget with the cash method of accounting for most non-credit expenditures. Notably, the balance of the MMIF does not constrain FHA from fulfilling its existing obligations. Like all federal credit programs, the FHA's mortgage insurance possesses permanent and indefinite budget authority to draw funds from the U.S. Treasury under the Federal Credit Reform Act of 1990 (FCRA).

In recent years, the MMIF balance has fallen sharply because of higher-than-expected losses from defaults. To prevent a negative balance from arising at the end of fiscal year 2013, the Treasury made an intragovernmental transfer of $1.7 billion to the MMIF. The capital reserve balance was $0 after that transfer. All told, the position of the fund is now $73 billion less than it would have been had the

Figure 1.1: FHA Share of Purchase Loan Originations

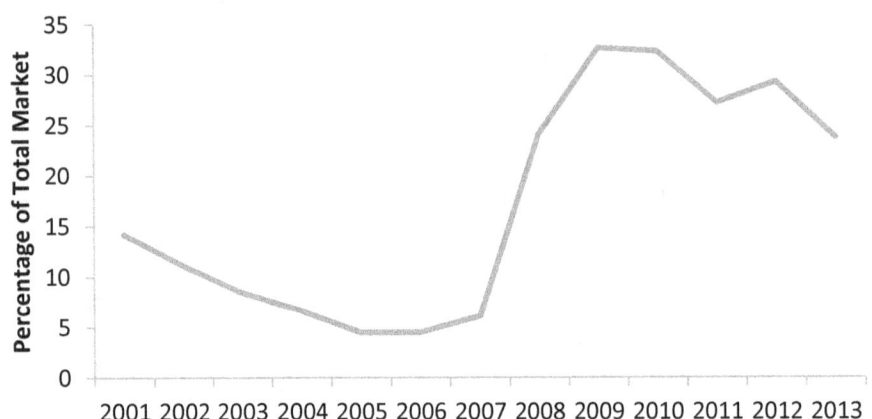

Note: 2013 share through first three quarters. Share measured by loan count.

Source: FHA-Insured Single-Family Mortgage Market Share Report, 2009 through 2013.

Figure 1.2: FHA and National Average Serious Delinquency Rates

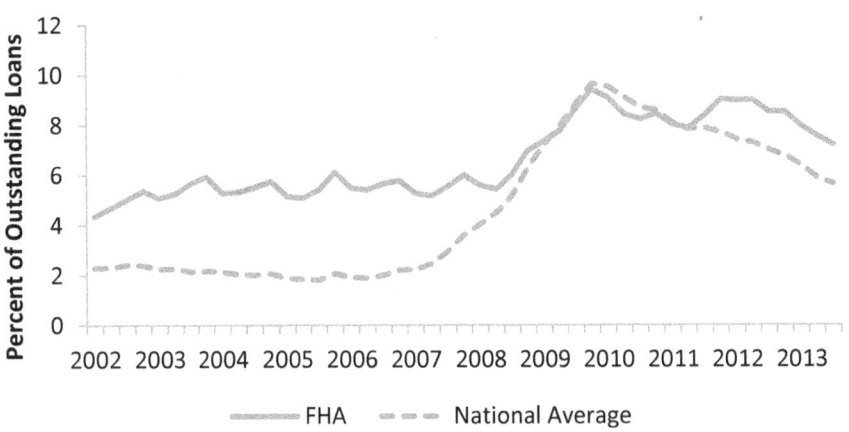

Notes: Serious Delinquency includes 90-day delinquency and foreclosure inventory.

Source: Mortgage Bankers Association National Delinquency Survey, 2005 through 2013.

originally estimated costs and fee income for the 1992 to 2013 cohorts prevailed, CBO estimates from the initial and reestimated subsidy rates reported in the *Fiscal Year 2015 Federal Credit Supplement* (2014).[1]

The initial surplus and subsequent deterioration in the value of the MMIF were reflected in the federal budget as, respectively, initial budgetary savings and subsequent budgetary outlays. Under FCRA, the estimated lifetime savings or cost of each cohort of loans that FHA guarantees are recorded in the budget in the year the loans are disbursed. (A cohort is the set of loans that FHA guarantees under its budget authority for a particular fiscal year.) The lifetime savings or cost is calculated as the present discounted value of all cash flows associated with the loan guarantees, discounted to the year of loan origination at Treasury rates of interest. FHA annually updates its estimates of the lifetime cost of previous cohorts' guarantee obligations that remain in effect. The change in estimated costs resulting from that update—the reestimate—is reflected in the deficit in the year the update is made. The annual reestimates reflect actual cash flows, as well as changes in the macroeconomic outlook, housing market conditions, and modeling choices that affect projections of future cash flows. The historic downturn in the housing market and upsurge in default losses led FHA to revise its estimated subsidy costs upward by a substantial amount. The upward revisions to FHA's estimated costs are largest for the 2001 to 2010 cohorts.[2] FHA's capital reserve balance reflects the cumulative effect of those revisions plus any interest credited to the balance of the account.

This working paper describes how FHA's mortgage guarantees are accounted for in the federal budget, and it presents CBO's independent projections of the subsidy costs for FHA's 1992 to 2015 cohorts and the contributions of those guarantees to FHA's capital reserve. As part of its baseline projections, CBO routinely assesses the budgetary cost of FHA's loan guarantees for the cohort that will be issued in the next fiscal year, but CBO does not routinely reestimate the costs of previously issued loan guarantees or estimate the status of FHA's capital reserve. CBO instead uses OMB's official estimates and reestimates of the cost of loans after they have been issued. Thus, the information presented in this paper supplements CBO's regular estimates by providing the agency's updated assessment of the costs of previous cohorts of loan guarantees and by conveying the uncertainty surrounding those estimated costs.

CBO estimates the 30-year lifetime performance of the loans in the 1992 to 2015 cohorts by combining each cohort's historical performance with dynamic simulations of the model presented in this paper. Those estimates allow subsidy rates (the lifetime cost as calculated under FCRA expressed as a percentage of the loan amounts insured, combining realized past and expected future performance) to be calculated for each cohort. CBO regularly uses variations of the model to estimate the subsidy rates for new FHA loan cohorts and to evaluate the impact of mortgage policies affecting FHA.

CBO estimates that the overall FCRA subsidy rate for the 1992 through 2015 cohorts will be negative 0.5 percent of the total volume of loans guaranteed.[3] That estimate implies that, under the rules prescribed by

---

[1] The Federal Credit Supplement is published by OMB and provides summary information about federal credit programs.

[2] For more detail, see Congressional Budget Office (2013b).

[3] The estimates presented in this paper are based on the economic assumptions in *The Budget and Economic Outlook: 2014 to 2024* (CBO 2014) and *The 2013 Long-Term Budget Outlook* (CBO 2013a); CBO has since released updated economic projections.

FCRA, those loan guarantees will produce net savings for taxpayers over their lifetimes.[4] Considering only the 1992 to 2013 cohorts, which are reflected in the value of the MMIF at the end of fiscal year 2013, the estimated average subsidy rate is 0.1 percent. Those cohorts' estimated contribution to FHA's capital reserve is positive $3.1 billion. That total does not include a $4.3 billion transfer to the financing account of the Home Equity Conversion Mortgage (HECM) program that occurred at the end of fiscal year 2013. (Although the HECM program is part of FHA's MMIF, the HECM program has substantially different characteristics than FHA's non-HECM mortgage guarantees and is therefore not included in CBO's analysis.) CBO estimates that the 2014 and 2015 cohorts will have an average subsidy rate of negative 5.5 percent under FCRA accounting, which would contribute $16 billion to FHA's capital reserves over the next two years.

Those estimates reflect a combination of realized gains and losses to date and CBO's projections of uncertain future gains and losses. The 1992 to 2013 cohorts of loan guarantees are projected to contribute between negative $28 billion and positive $26 billion to FHA's capital reserves in 90 percent of model simulations. The 2014 and 2015 cohorts are expected to contribute between $8 billion and $24 billion to FHA's capital reserves in 90 percent of model simulations.

Finally, the paper presents an alternative estimate of FHA's subsidy costs using a fair-value methodology, which reflects the economic resources committed through FHA's loan guarantees more comprehensively than the FCRA methodology. The fair-value methodology differs from the FCRA methodology by incorporating a cost for market risk—the cost a private investor would require to bear the risks associated with FHA's loan guarantees.[5] CBO estimates that the remaining cash flows associated with the 1992 to 2013 cohorts have a fair value cost of $63.4 billion, implying that a private investor would require compensation of $63.4 billion to assume FHA's remaining fee income and liabilities associated with those cohorts. Similarly, CBO estimates that the cash flows associated with the 2014 and 2015 cohorts have a fair-value cost of $2 billion. Thus, accounting explicitly for the cost of the market risk associated with those cohorts eliminates the cost savings implied by the FCRA methodology and results in substantial estimated net costs.

2. Accounting for the Cost of FHA's Mortgage Guarantees

FCRA requires that the costs of FHA's mortgage insurance, like other federal credit programs, be accounted for on an accrual basis following FCRA procedures. An alternative approach to FCRA procedures, known as fair value, would provide more comprehensive estimates of the cost of that insurance.

2.1 Accrual Accounting Under FCRA

In accrual accounting, expenses and revenues are recorded when the obligation is incurred, rather than when payments are made or received. Thus, the estimated lifetime costs or savings stemming from new federal loans or loan guarantees are recorded in the federal budget in the year in which the loans are

---

[4] Administrative costs are not included in calculations of the loan guarantees' effect on the budget.

[5] For a more detailed comparison of FCRA and fair-value accounting, see Congressional Budget Office (2012).

disbursed, with the government's spending expressed as the present value of net federal cash payments over the life of the loans or loan guarantees. (That present value is often referred to as the subsidy for those loans or guarantees.) In the case of FHA's loan guarantees, the net cash payments are the estimated claim payments minus recoveries and fees. Federal administrative costs for FCRA programs are accounted for separately (on a cash basis) and do not affect estimated subsidies. To compute the subsidy, program cash flows are discounted to the date of disbursement using a sequence of interest rates for each year of cash flow corresponding to the interest rate on Treasury securities of corresponding maturity. (For example, the projected yield on Treasury securities maturing in two years is used to discount cash flows two years from the disbursement date, a three-year Treasury rate for cash flows three years from disbursement, and so on.)

To facilitate accrual accounting in a largely cash accounting system, the federal budget uses a capital reserve account and a financing account to reconcile the budgetary effects of loans and loan guarantees with the cash flows. When FHA makes new loan guarantees, the federal budget records an outlay in the amount of the FCRA subsidy. Because the initially estimated subsidy rate for FHA's loan guarantees has been negative in each year since FCRA's accounting rules were put into place, the originally recorded outlays have also been negative. The estimated negative subsidy is recorded in FHA's capital reserve account in recognition that future receipts are expected to be greater than the insurance payouts the program is expected to make. Over time, the capital reserve balance accrues interest and reflects revisions to the estimated subsidies of prior loan guarantees. In the event of an upward credit subsidy reestimate, which implies that a cohort is expected to be more costly than previously anticipated, funds are transferred from the capital reserve account to the financing account, which is the budgetary account that tracks the federal cash payments in the program. Therefore, the value of the capital reserve account for FHA's mortgage guarantees should equal the sum of all previous cohorts' reestimated subsidy costs plus accumulated interest on those amounts, minus occasional transfers to accounts associated with FHA's HECM program.[6]

Table 2.1 presents an approach to calculating the value of the capital reserve account attributable to FHA's loan programs (excluding the HECM program) from the reestimated historical credit subsidy rates reported in the *Fiscal Year 2015 Federal Credit Supplement*. The reestimated subsidy rates are multiplied by the dollar volumes of loans guaranteed to calculate each cohort's contribution to the value of the capital reserve account before interest is accumulated. Cohorts with negative estimated subsidy rates make a positive contribution to the value of the account, and cohorts with positive estimated subsidy rates make a negative contribution. For the calculation in Table 2.1, CBO used the prevailing rate on one-year Treasury securities to approximate the rate of interest that has been earned on the account; that approach is only a rough approximation because FHA has invested funds from the capital reserve account into nonmarketable Treasury securities with a range of maturities. Adding the accumulated interest to the reestimated subsidy rates and subtracting the $4.3 billion transfer to the HECM financing account made in fiscal year 2013 results in an implied value of negative $1 billion in the capital reserve account as of the end of fiscal year 2013. That implied value differs from the $0 reported by FHA, but the discrepancy is less than 0.04 percent of the $2.8 trillion of loan guarantees FHA made in the 1992 to 2013 cohorts.

---

[6] For instance, in fiscal year 2013, FHA made a transfer of $4.3 billion from the capital reserve account to the HECM financing account.

Table 2.1: Calculating the Contribution of FHA's Loan Guarantees to the Capital Reserve Account[1]
End of Fiscal Year 2013

Cohort	Reestimated Subsidy Rate[2] (%)	Dollar Volume[2] ($ bil.)	Noninterest Contribution to Capital Reserve Account ($ bil.)	Average One-Year Treasury Rate from Cohort Origination to Present[3] (%)	Estimated Accrued Interest ($ bil.)	Total Contribution to Capital Reserve Account ($ bil.)
(a)	(b)	(c)	(d) = -(b)*(c)	(e)	(f)[4]	(g) = (d) + (f)
1992	-3.22	43.4	1.4	3.2	1.4	2.8
1993	-2.66	71.6	1.9	3.2	1.7	3.6
1994	-1.80	82.4	1.5	3.2	1.2	2.7
1995	-0.74	41.0	0.3	3.0	0.2	0.5
1996	-1.05	64.2	0.7	2.9	0.4	1.1
1997	-1.01	67.0	0.7	2.7	0.4	1.1
1998	-1.44	93.3	1.3	2.5	0.6	2.0
1999	-1.25	111.8	1.4	2.4	0.6	2.0
2000	0.25	84.9	-0.2	2.2	-0.1	-0.3
2001	0.16	121.6	-0.2	1.9	-0.1	-0.2
2002	0.49	131.4	-0.6	1.8	-0.1	-0.8
2003	1.24	116.0	-1.4	1.8	-0.3	-1.7
2004	2.73	107.6	-2.9	1.8	-0.6	-3.5
2005	8.13	58.0	-4.7	1.8	-0.8	-5.5
2006	8.50	51.8	-4.4	1.5	-0.5	-4.9
2007	12.00	56.5	-6.8	1.0	-0.4	-7.2
2008	8.33	171.8	-14.3	0.5	-0.4	-14.7
2009	2.03	330.5	-6.7	0.3	-0.1	-6.8
2010	-0.50	297.6	1.5	0.2	0.0	1.5
2011	-3.10	217.7	6.8	0.2	0.0	6.8
2012	-4.88	213.2	10.4	0.1	0.0	10.4
2013	-6.02	240.0	14.4	0.1	0.0	14.5
Less FY 2013 transfer to HECM Financing Account						-4.3
Total		2,773.2	-0.1		3.4	-1.0

Notes:

1. The calculations exclude the contributions of the HECM guarantees except for the FY 2013 transfer to the HECM financing account.

2. As reported in table 8 of the Fiscal Year 2015 Federal Credit Supplement.

3. Calculated from data reported in Federal Reserve data release H.15.

4. For convenience the calculation of accrued interest assumes that loans are originated evenly throughout the year, so the formula for accrued interest is given by: $(f) = (d)*[(1+(e))^{2013.5-(a)}-1]$.

FHA's capital reserve account is operationally important because FHA is required to maintain a capital ratio of at least 2 percent of the amortized insurance in force (i.e., the present balance of outstanding loans that are guaranteed by FHA).[7] Since 2009, FHA has not met that requirement, and the account balance stood at $0 at the end of fiscal year 2013. Since 2009, FHA has sought to improve its financial position by increasing fees and imposing more stringent loan qualification requirements. In the *2013 Actuarial Review of the MMIF,* the Department of Housing and Urban Development (2013a) estimated that because of savings from FHA's future cohorts, the capital reserve balance will reach the statutorily required 2 percent ratio in fiscal year 2016.

The balance in the capital reserve account provides a snapshot of the cumulative performance of FHA's single-family mortgage insurance program, but reliance on the measure has drawbacks:

- The balance in the capital reserve account can be misinterpreted as a measure of FHA's solvency or as a measure of real resources available to offset additional spending by the federal government. FCRA provides FHA with the authority to draw on the Treasury for additional funds even if FHA's capital reserves are insufficient, so FHA is never at risk of insolvency. Furthermore, the budgetary savings of FHA loan guarantees under FCRA is reported as an offset to other spending in the year of loan disbursement and is not available to offset spending in future periods.

- Reconciling the balance in the capital reserve account with reestimated credit subsidy rates is not a straightforward process for two reasons. First, the rate at which the balance in the capital reserve account accrues interest is not readily apparent. Second, transfers from the capital reserve account to the HECM financing account and from the Treasury to the capital reserve account weaken the link between the capital reserve account and the cumulative subsidies.

- The requirement that FHA satisfy a minimum capital ratio for the capital reserve account weakens the connection between FHA's insurance pricing for new borrowers and the cost of the risks they pose. The requirement leads the FHA to raise fees when the estimated costs for previous cohorts are revised upward. Unlike private financial institutions, FHA cannot issue capital, so FHA's only mechanism for increasing the balance in its capital reserve account is to record negative subsidies on new mortgage guarantees. Therefore, new borrowers must pay higher fees for losses that have been incurred (or are projected to be incurred) on guarantees for previous borrowers. Conversely, FHA can charge—and historically has charged—lower fees when previous cohorts perform better than initially expected, allowing new borrowers to benefit from previous borrowers' performance.

---

[7] This requirement is included in the Cranston-Gonzalez National Affordable Housing Act of 1990. For more information, see Government Accountability Office (2013).

Figure 2.1: Capital Reserve Ratio of the MMIF Excluding HECMs

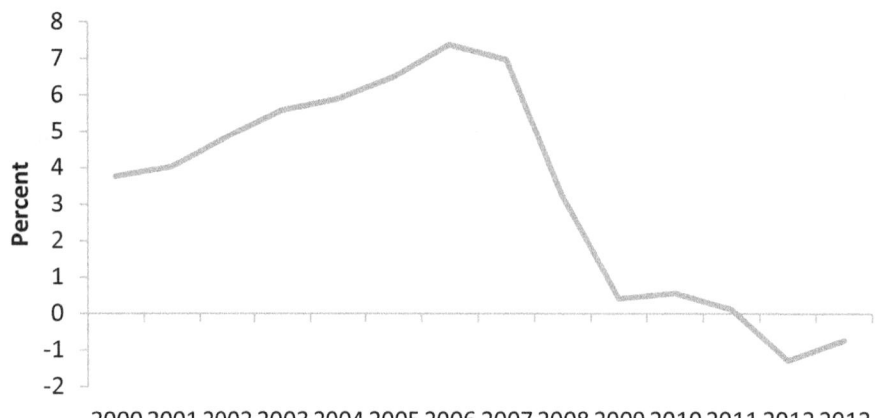

Notes: Capital reserve ratio calculated by dividing the balance of the fund by the amortized insurance-in-force. HECMs are Home Equity Conversion Mortgages.
Source: Department of Housing and Urban Development (multiple years).

2.2 An Alternative Fair-Value Approach

A broader shortcoming of the current budgetary treatment of FHA is that the FCRA-based subsidy estimates reported in the budget and underlying the capital reserve account do not provide a comprehensive measure of the economic cost of the FHA's programs. Under the fair-value approach, estimates more comprehensively reflect the economic cost of the risks posed. Specifically, fair-value estimates are based on market values in a well-functioning market. The estimates are based on actual market prices when markets are functioning well and prices are available, and on approximations of market prices when directly comparable figures are unavailable. Investors in risky assets such as mortgages add a risk premium to the rates observed on Treasury securities to discount mortgage cash flows. Those risk premiums are reflected in the privately determined prices for mortgages and mortgage guarantees.

The fair-value approach differs from the FCRA approach by incorporating those risk premiums into the discount rates used to convert projected cash payments and receipts to present values. The projected cash payments and receipts are identical under the FCRA and fair-value approaches; only the discount rates used to convert those amounts to a present value differ. If subsidies for the FHA's loan guarantees had been computed using fair-value accounting procedures rather than FCRA procedures, subsidy savings would have been significantly smaller and in many years the subsidies would have been reported as costs. The reported value of FHA's capital reserve would also be substantially lower if estimated on the basis of the fair-value subsidies.

Incorporating the risk premium more fully reflects the opportunity cost to the government of the risks the government assumes when it extends credit.[8] Thus, by ignoring the market risk premium, FCRA

---

[8] The risk premium is generally recognized as compensation for the cost of market risk, which is one component of financial risk. Much of the risk of financial investments can be avoided by diversifying a portfolio; market risk is the component of risk that remains even after a portfolio has been diversified as much as possible. It arises because most investments tend to perform

accounting creates a budgetary incentive to expand FHA's guarantee program beyond the scale that would be chosen if the budget reflected comprehensive estimates of the costs of the program. FCRA accounting also lowers the reported costs of those loan guarantees relative to grants or benefit payments with the same cost when measured at market prices, which could distort policymakers' decisions.

However, some analysts have expressed concerns about potential drawbacks of using the fair-value approach in federal budgeting, for FHA and more generally.[9] One concern is that fair-value estimates of the costs of federal credit programs include costs that will not be paid directly by the federal government if actual cash flows turn out to match expected cash flows. Suppose that the cash flows from a cohort of loan guarantees turned out to match CBO's expectations, and that future Treasury rates turned out to match the rates that CBO used in constructing FCRA estimates. If there were no offsetting changes elsewhere in the budget, that cohort would decrease future federal debt by roughly the future value of its estimated cost savings on a FCRA basis instead of increasing future federal debt by the future value of the estimated cost on a fair-value basis. Estimates of the costs of noncredit programs are, like FCRA estimates, indicators of the effect of those programs on future federal debt (excluding debt service costs). That line of reasoning might suggest that, by increasing the estimated budgetary cost of credit programs, the fair-value approach makes comparisons with estimated costs for noncredit programs more difficult and puts credit programs at a disadvantage in the competition for budgetary resources.

In fact, in some cases, using the more comprehensive estimates produced under the fair-value approach makes estimates of the costs loan guarantees *more* comparable with estimates of the costs of other credit programs and noncredit programs. For example, when comparing a proposal to provide loan guarantees for home mortgages with a proposal for grants to help people reduce the down payments on their mortgages, using a fair-value estimate for the loan guarantees allows for a more accurate comparison with the estimated cost of the grants. However, in some other cases, using fair-value estimates for credit programs reduces the comparability of those estimates with estimates for noncredit programs. For example, when comparing the proposal to provide those loan guarantees to a proposal that would provide additional unemployment insurance benefits, using a fair-value estimate for the proposal with loan guarantees produces a less accurate comparison because unemployment insurance imposes market risk on the government, risk that is not reflected in a standard estimate of the budgetary cost of that insurance.

Another concern is that moving to a system of fair-value accounting would entail additional effort and expense for FHA and for OMB, which oversees the process of estimating the costs of federal loan guarantees. Start-up expenses of implementing the fair-value approach would include funding for additional training and possible expansion of staff, for redesign of procedures and account structures, and for development of models and approaches for producing estimates. Even over the long term, some additional resources would probably be needed because of the greater complexity of producing fair-value estimates.

---

relatively poorly when the economy is weak and relatively well when the economy is strong. People value income from investments more when the economy is weak and incomes are relatively low, and so they assign a higher cost to losses that occur during economic downturns. The higher cost of losses in bad times (as well as a lower cost of losses in good times) is captured in the cost of market risk. In federal programs that have market risk, the cost is effectively passed along to taxpayers or beneficiaries of government programs because they bear the consequences of the government's financial losses.

[9] The following discussion draws on Congressional Budget Office (2014b).

An added complication is that recording a positive instead of negative subsidy rate would result in initial budgetary outlays instead of savings, meaning that each new cohort of loans would—at least initially—draw on rather than add to FHA's capital reserves. Although FHA could raise the fees it charges to reduce those fair-value subsidies, raising fees to achieve a substantial negative fair-value subsidy would be difficult due to competition from the private sector. Thus, fair-value accounting could hinder setting fees to accumulate a positive capital reserve ratio, as FHA is required to do under current law.

However, in place of a capital reserve requirement, the estimated fair-value subsidy rates could be used to guide pricing on new loan guarantees. For instance, FHA could set fees to target a particular subsidy rate in every year. Under that approach, if unexpected economic developments resulted in different realized subsidies than initially projected for previous cohorts, that outcome would have no direct impact on pricing for new borrowers. And FHA's permanent and indefinite budget authority would allow it to meet its obligations in the event of larger-than-expected losses (as under current law). Switching to fair-value accounting would not on its own affect the economic cost of FHA insurance to the government; it would only affect how comprehensively that cost was reflected in the budget.

As a general matter, the usefulness of different approaches for constructing estimates of the costs of federal policies depends on the purposes for which those estimates are used. Fair-value estimates may be less useful than FCRA estimates in projecting the average budgetary effects of programs that provide credit assistance, but projecting such effects is not the only, or even the primary, purpose of cost estimates. Cost estimates are tools that policymakers can use to make tradeoffs between different policies that work toward a particular policy goal. By taking into account how the public assesses financial risks as expressed through market prices, fair-value estimates may be more useful than FCRA estimates in helping policymakers understand tradeoffs between policies that involve such risks.

3. Modeling Mortgage Cash Flows

A model of mortgage cash flows is central to estimating the budgetary costs of FHA's mortgage insurance. The cash flows associated with a mortgage guarantee depend on the fees collected over the life of the loan and any claim payments minus recoveries resulting from a default. FHA charges borrowers both up-front and annual fees for its mortgage insurance. The fee schedule for the loans, described in Table 3.1, is specified in the mortgage contract, but actual fees collected will depend on whether and when the loan terminates through default or prepayment. Likewise, claim payments and recoveries will depend on the timing of a potential default. Therefore, models of mortgage default and prepayment, a model of loss rates conditional on default, and forecasts of macroeconomic conditions are necessary to predict the cash flows associated with FHA's loan guarantees.

Mortgage default and prepayment decisions involve both financial and behavioral aspects. Early research applied options pricing theory, in recognition that a mortgage contains implicit put and call options.[10] On a mortgage without recourse, default can be interpreted as a *put option*. By defaulting, the borrower can relinquish (or "put") the house to the mortgage holder instead of paying off the mortgage. The mortgage

---

[10] Kau and Keenan (1995) and Deng, Quigley, and Van Order (2000) survey the default option pricing literature.

Table 3.1: FHA Single-Family Mortgage Insurance Fee Schedule

Cohort[1]	Fully Underwritten		Streamline Refinance	
	Upfront Premium	Annual Premium[2]	Upfront Premium	Annual Premium[2]
1992	3.80%	0.50%	3.80%	0.50%
1993	3.00%	0.50%	3.00%	0.50%
1994	2.63%	0.50%	2.63%	0.50%
1995	2.25%	0.50%	2.25%	0.50%
1996	2.25%	0.50%	2.25%	0.50%
1997	2.25%	0.50%	2.25%	0.50%
1998	2.25%	0.50%	2.25%	0.50%
1999	2.25%	0.50%	2.25%	0.50%
2000	2.25%	0.50%	2.25%	0.50%
2001	1.69%	0.50%	1.69%	0.50%
2002	1.50%	0.50%	1.50%	0.50%
2003	1.50%	0.50%	1.50%	0.50%
2004	1.50%	0.50%	1.50%	0.50%
2005	1.50%	0.50%	1.50%	0.50%
2006	1.50%	0.50%	1.50%	0.50%
2007	1.50%	0.50%	1.50%	0.50%
2008	1.50%	0.50%	1.50%	0.50%
2009	1.75%	0.55%	1.50%	0.55%
2010	2.00%	0.55%	1.88%	0.55%
2011	1.00%	1.03%	1.00%	1.03%
2012	1.38%	1.20%	0.75%	1.00%
2013[3]	1.75%	1.30%	0.01%	0.55%
2014[3]	1.75%	1.35%	0.01%	0.55%
2015[3]	1.75%	1.35%	0.01%	0.55%

Notes:

1. Weighted average fees are presented in cases where fees were changed mid-year.

2. FHA loans have historically been eligible for annual premium cancellation once certain conditions relating to loan-to-value ratio and age of loan have been met. From 2001 to 2013, loans were typically eligible for annual premium cancellation after five years if the loan-to-value ratio was less than 78 percent. Beginning in June 2013, loans with an original loan-to-value ratio greater than 90 percent are not eligible for annual premium cancellation, and other loans become eligible after 11 years.

3. Streamline refinances of loans originally endorsed on or before May 31, 2009, are eligible for the reduced premiums shown in the table. Streamline refinances of loans endorsed on or after June 1, 2009, are charged the same premiums as fully underwritten loans. Streamline refinances in the 2012 to 2015 cohorts include loans originally endorsed both before and after June 1, 2009.

holder effectively pays the mortgage balance in exchange for release from the contract. When the value of the house is sufficiently below the amount owed on the mortgage (i.e. when the borrower has negative equity) exercising the put option is valuable to the borrower. Prepayment by refinancing serves as a *call option*—the right for the borrower to buy out (or "call") his mortgage without penalty for the amount of the unpaid principal balance. The prepayment option is more valuable when market interest rates are below the current interest rate on the mortgage, allowing the borrower to take a new mortgage at a lower rate.

A narrow interpretation of those put and call options ignores important financial frictions that prevent their exercise, including the transactions costs and underwriting constraints associated with refinancing a mortgage as well as the costs of defaulting, such as legal expenses and a potential reduction in future credit access.[11] Furthermore, a growing body of literature finds that many borrowers do not take advantage of the options because of lack of information, moral aversion, and other behavioral biases.[12] Nonetheless, an important insight of the options theory is that if there is some probability that house prices will increase sharply, then waiting to default may be more valuable than defaulting immediately. Likewise, if there is some probability that mortgage rates will continue to decline, then waiting to prepay may be more valuable than doing so immediately.

Empirical research has focused on the role that trigger events, such as unemployment and divorce, play in decisions to prepay and default. Clapp and others (2001) and Clapp, Deng, and An (2006) distinguish empirically between prepayments motivated by the value of the call option (refinancing), and those motivated by household mobility (for example, moving to find work). Bajari, Chu, and Park (2010) show theoretically and empirically that credit constraints, such as the inability to qualify for a new mortgage or to borrow money outside of the mortgage market, have predictive power for the mortgage default decision that cannot be explained by option value. The literature often refers to borrowers in that situation as being liquidity-constrained.

Liquidity constraints appear to affect the default decision. Several recent papers, including Elul and others (2010) and Pennington-Cross and Ho (2010), find support for the "double trigger hypothesis," which posits that defaults occur with much higher probability when the borrower faces both negative equity and credit constraints. The combination of those conditions makes it more difficult for such borrowers to avoid default. Bhutta, Dokko, and Shan (2010) estimate that, for borrowers who default in the absence of credit constraints, the average level of equity is negative 62 percent. They find that many borrowers are willing to continue paying the mortgage on a home with negative equity if they are able to do so and that the option theory of default on its own explains only one-fifth of the defaults in their dataset, with the double trigger hypothesis explaining the remainder.

Statistical models of mortgage termination typically employ what is known as a duration model to estimate a loan's probabilities of default and prepayment in each period, conditional on the loan having remained active until that period. A loan can terminate before maturity either by default or by prepayment, but not both. Therefore, it is appropriate to model default and prepayment as "competing

---

[11] See Deng, Quigley, and Van Order (2000), and Ambrose, Capone, and Deng (2001).

[12] See, for instance, Guiso, Sapienza, and Zingales (2013).

risks," so that the probabilities of survival, default, and prepayment add up to 100 percent for each period that the loan remains active. Researchers have most often estimated such models using the Cox proportional hazards model and the multinomial logit model. Both models have been shown to perform well (see, for example, Clapp and others (2001)).

CBO uses a multinomial logit duration model to analyze FHA borrowers' default and prepayment behavior. The model builds on the theoretical and empirical work described above in order to capture option-theoretic and liquidity-related determinants of a borrower's likelihood of default and prepayment. The model includes measures of the loan-to-value ratio (LTV) and interest rates to capture implications from options theory, along with measures of borrower creditworthiness such as credit score and debt-to-income ratio to reflect borrower liquidity.

CBO also models FHA's expected losses given default and expected fee income as follows:

- *Loss Given Default (LGD)*. CBO employs ordinary least squares (OLS) to model FHA's loss given default, consistent with most previous studies. For recent examples, see Qi and Yang (2009) and Department of Housing and Urban Development (2013a). Qi and Zhao (2011) compare OLS to other methods and find that OLS is generally appropriate in the context of the mortgage market.
- *Fee Income*. FHA's fees are specified in the mortgage contract and have varied over the time period CBO considers. Borrowers pay up-front fees and annual premiums, which are tied to the unpaid principal balance of the loan. The annual premium may terminate when certain conditions are met. The estimates of FHA's fee income are consistent with CBO's expectations for the performance of the underlying loans.

4. Probabilities of Default and Prepayment

Most loans pay mortgage insurance premiums to FHA while they remain active. A termination through prepayment ends that income stream, while a termination through default generates costs for FHA in the form of a claim payment. Therefore, predicting the timing of prepayments and defaults is central to modeling FHA's cash flows. Consistent with several papers in the literature, CBO uses a multinomial logit duration model to estimate default and prepayment rates for FHA loans.[13]

4.1 Statistical Model
Each quarter that a loan remains active provides one observation in the statistical model. Let j index the three possible outcomes for a loan that begins quarter t as an active loan, with $j = 0$ indicating that the loan remains active at the end of quarter t, $j = 1$ indicating that the loan defaults in quarter t, and $j = 2$ indicating that the loan prepays in quarter t. Additionally, define P_{ijt} as the probability that loan i will experience outcome j in quarter t, conditional on having been active at the beginning of the quarter. Then the system of equations

---

[13] See, for instance, Clapp and others (2006), Elul and others (2010), and Department of Housing and Urban Development (2013a).

$$P_{ijt} = \frac{e^{X_{it}\beta_j}}{1 + e^{X_{it}\beta_1} + e^{X_{it}\beta_2}} , \quad j = 1, 2$$
$$P_{i0t} = 1 - P_{i1t} - P_{i2t},$$

forms a multinomial logit model of conditional default and prepayment probabilities, where X_{it} is a vector of loan characteristics for loan i at quarter t, and β_1 and β_2 are the vectors of parameters to be estimated. Defining d_{ijt} as an indicator equal to 1 if loan i experiences outcome j in period t, and T_i as the number of quarters loan i is observed in the dataset, the log-likelihood function of the model can be written as

$$\ln L = \sum_{i=1}^{N} \sum_{j=0}^{2} \sum_{t=1}^{T_i} d_{ijt} \ln(P_{ijt}).$$

The log-likelihood and the parameters β_1 and β_2 can be estimated by maximum likelihood methods using standard statistical software.

4.2 Data

The dataset underlying the analysis in this paper was drawn from a random sample of 3.7 million loans that FHA guaranteed between 1990 and 2010. In addition to that random sample, FHA provided data on the entire universe of defaulted loans; those additional loans are included in the analysis of loss given default but not in the analysis of default and prepayment probabilities. The analysis considers 30-year fixed rate mortgages because they constitute the bulk of FHA's business. A smaller estimation sample of 500,000 loans that contained all essential data was randomly drawn from the set of loans. The dataset was converted to a quarterly panel for the statistical estimation, meaning that each loan contributes an observation for each quarter of its active life.

FHA does not collect a full range of data on streamline refinances, which are refinance loans of previously originated FHA mortgages. FHA has reduced underwriting and documentation requirements for streamline refinances, so many streamline refinances lack essential data and are therefore excluded from the regression analysis. (Section 6.1 describes how the costs of streamline refinances were projected and the implications of excluding them from the estimation sample. The robustness of the approach is discussed in the Appendix.)

Only loans for which FHA reports a claim from the mortgage lender are considered defaults in the analysis. For those loans, this analysis defines the date of default as the date of the last mortgage payment plus one quarter, corresponding to a delinquency of 90 days. A loan ends in prepayment if the borrower pays the outstanding balance of the loan in that quarter.

Because foreclosures can take a substantial amount of time to complete, especially in the wake of the recent financial crisis, many loans that will eventually end in foreclosure are not reported as such in the data sample. As a result of that reporting lag, default and foreclosure data are not reliable after the fourth quarter of 2009. Therefore, the estimation sample was censored at that date for the analysis of default and prepayment.

The loan characteristics used as explanatory variables in the statistical model can be divided into dynamic variables, with values that change over the life of the loan, and static variables, with values that are fixed over the life of the loan. The variables are described in detail in Table 4.1.

In order to account for their potentially nonlinear effects on default and prepayment probabilities, most of the continuous explanatory variables are recoded into categorical variables that take the value one if the variable is within a certain range and zero otherwise. For instance, the model contains five separate binary variables that correspond to loan-to-value ratios less than 80 percent, 80 to 90 percent, 90 to 95 percent, 95 to 97 percent, and greater than 97 percent. A variable takes the value one if the observation's loan-to-value ratio falls within the specified limits and zero otherwise.

Table 4.2 presents descriptive statistics for select variables. The average loan-to-value (LTV) ratio in the sample at origination is 94.9 percent, while the average original LTV of defaulted loans is 96 percent. The average borrower credit score for all loans is 669, which is higher than the average on defaulted loans of 618. The average interest rate on all loans is significantly lower than the interest rate on loans that default or prepay. The average age of a loan at default is 12.5 quarters, and the average age at prepayment is 15.6 quarters.

4.3 Results

Table 4.3 displays the results of estimating the multinomial logit model. Panel A displays the results for conditional default probabilities and panel B displays the results for conditional prepayment probabilities. Because the effects of the explanatory variables in a logistic regression model are highly nonlinear, it can be difficult to interpret the coefficients of the estimated model in terms of the size of the estimated effects. Therefore, Table 4.3 also displays estimated marginal effects for a loan that has been active for 20 quarters, with explanatory variables at their sample averages. The marginal effects represent the effect of a one-unit increase in the explanatory variable on the estimated quarterly conditional probability of default or prepayment, holding the other variables constant. For the categorical variables, the marginal effects are expressed relative to the base—or omitted—category. The marginal effects are displayed as a proportion of the sample average conditional probabilities of default or prepayment. Therefore, a marginal effect of 0.1 indicates that a change from the base category to the given category is associated with a 10 percent increase in the conditional probability of default or prepayment.

The results for default behavior are generally consistent with theory and previous research. The baseline probability of default increases sharply over the first two years of a loan's life before declining gradually thereafter. The probability of negative equity has a major effect on the probability of default. The marginal effects imply that an increase in the probability of negative equity from the range of 5 to 10 percent to the range of 10 to 15 percent increases the probability of default by 27 percent. A higher borrower credit score significantly reduces the probability of default. Moving from a borrower FICO score in the 659 to 679 range to the 679 to 719 range reduces the probability of default by roughly 10 percent. A higher loan-to-value ratio at origination has a mixed association with the probability of default; a rise in LTV from below 80 percent to the 80 to 90 percent range increases the probability of default by about 15 percent, but at higher LTVs a rise in LTV is associated with a lower probability of default relative to the peak, holding other variables constant. Differences in borrower attributes unobserved in the dataset may account for that result, for instance, in cases where lenders require borrowers with the highest

Table 4.1: Variable Definitions for Default and Prepayment Model

Static Variables [1]

Variable	Coding[2]	Description
Loan-to-value ratio (LTV)	Categorical	The ratio of the original mortgage amount to the value of the mortgaged property at the time of loan origination.
Borrower credit score (FICO)	Categorical	The lowest decision score across borrowers on a loan application, where each borrower's credit score is the median of reported scores. Available after May 2004.
Debt-to-income ratio (DTI)	Categorical	The borrower's debt-to-income ratio at the time of loan origination, also known as the back-end ratio.
Loan size ratio	Categorical	The ratio of the original mortgage amount to the original amount of the average mortgage guaranteed by Fannie Mae or Freddie Mac originated in the same state and year.
Refinance	Indicator	An indicator for whether the loan is a purchase loan or a refinance. Refinance status does not depend on whether the original loan was an FHA loan.
Outside downpayment source	Indicator	An indicator for whether the borrower used an outside source of funds for the down payment.
Origination date	Indicator	Indicators for whether the loan's closing date was prior to October 1, 1994, or between October 1, 1994, and September 30, 1999.

Dynamic Variables [3]

Variable	Coding	Description
Age	Spline	The age of the loan in quarters. The linear spline function for age allows the baseline default and prepayment probabilities to vary flexibly over the life of the loan.
Probability of negative equity (PNEG)	Categorical	The probability that a borrower has negative equity in the home. It is included rather than the current loan-to-value ratio because the market value of the home after origination is not observed. PNEG is calculated according to the method of Deng, Quigley, and van Order (2000), which utilizes house price indices and measures of house price dispersion from the Federal Housing Finance Agency (FHFA) for the MSA or state in which the property is located.
Mortgage premium (MP)	Categorical	The present value of the savings a borrower would realize by refinancing into a conventional mortgage, considering interest rates and insurance premiums, as calculated by CBO and expressed as a percentage of the remaining balance of the loan.
Change in unemployment	Continuous	The yearly change in the unemployment rate of the state where the property is located.
Calendar quarter	Indicator	A set of indicators for the calendar quarter, to account for seasonal effects.

Notes:

1. Static variables have fixed values over the life of each loan.

2. The 'Coding' column describes how variables are entered into the statistical model. Variables coded as categorical enter the model as a set of binary variables that take the value one if the underlying variable falls within a specified range and zero otherwise. Variables coded as indicators take the value one if the observation satisfies the described criteria and zero otherwise. Variables coded as splines take continuous values defined by piecewise linear functions between a set of specified knot-points. Variables coded as continuous enter the statistical model without transformation.

3. Dynamic variables change values over the life of each loan.

Table 4.2: Descriptive Statistics for Default and Prepayment Model

Panel A: At Origination

Variable	All loans	Defaulted	Prepaid
Loan-to-Value Ratio[2]	94.9	96.0	95.0
	(5.3)	(3.9)	(5.3)
Borrower FICO Score[3]	669.0	617.7	663.0
	(65.4)	(60.2)	(66.7)
Interest Rate	7.0	7.5	7.6
	(1.4)	(1.2)	(1.2)
Mortgage Premium[4]	6.1	6.7	5.9
	(7.3)	(7.6)	(7.6)
Sample Size	500,000	29,729	299,595

Panel B: At 16 Quarters or Termination

Variable	Aged 16 quarters	Defaulted	Prepaid
Mortgage Premium[4]	9.00	11.62	13.19
	(8.84)	(8.94)	(8.26)
Age (quarters)	16	12.51	15.61
	-	(9.61)	(11.84)
Probability of Negative Equity[5]	0.11	0.21	0.10
	(0.16)	(0.22)	(0.16)
Sample Size	183,663	29,729	299,595

Notes:

1. Standard deviations are reported in parentheses.

2. Loan-to-Value Ratio is the ratio of the original mortgage amount to the value of the mortgaged property at the time of loan origination.

3. Borrower FICO score is the borrower's credit score as reported by FHA.

4. Mortgage premium approximates the present value of the savings a borrower would realize by refinancing into a conventional mortgage, as a percentage of the unpaid balance. See table 4.1 for a detailed description.

5. Probability of negative equity defined in the manner of Deng, Quigley, and van Order (2000).

LTVs to have other characteristics that offset their risk. Note, however, that many of the LTV category coefficients are statistically insignificant.

A higher mortgage premium is associated with a higher probability of default. That result is consistent with options pricing theory, which says that the default option becomes more valuable when the mortgage premium is higher, and with the idea that borrowers who do not refinance when market rates are much lower than their existing mortgage rate are more likely to experience financial distress and have difficulty refinancing. Moving from a mortgage premium in the range of negative 6 to positive 3 percent to the range of 3 to 9 percent increases the probability of default by 15 percent. As context for that result, increasing FHA's annual premium by 100 basis points with no possibility of cancellation increases the mortgage premium by an estimated 9.7 percent on a new loan with a note rate of 6 percent if conventional mortgage rates were also 6 percent. (That increase is smaller for an older loan.) Larger loan amounts tend to be associated with lower probabilities of default. Moving from a loan size ratio in the range of 50 to 60 percent to the range of 60 to 70 percent is associated with an 8 percent decrease in the probability of default.

The use of an outside source, often the seller or a non-profit organization, for a down payment increases the probability of default by 64 percent. The regression results also imply that refinance loans are more likely to default than purchase loans *conditional* on the other loan characteristics considered in the regression. Refinances tend to have substantially lower loan-to-value ratios than purchase loans, which means that refinances generally have a lower overall probability of default than purchase loans. The coefficients on the early origination periods are negative, implying that, holding their other characteristics constant, loans originated prior to fiscal year 2000 are less likely to default than loans originated later.

The debt-to-income ratio at origination has only a weak association with the probability of default, potentially because debt-to-income ratios are measured imprecisely in the data. One reason for that result may be that borrowers have little incentive to report income above the amount necessary to qualify for the mortgage. The weak association between the debt-to-income ratio and default is consistent with the conclusions of Foote and others (2009), who find that the debt-to-income ratio at mortgage origination is not a strong predictor of default in their data.

The change in the state unemployment rate has a slight negative correlation with defaults, with a one percentage point increase in the unemployment rate decreasing the probability of default by approximately 9 percent. The sign and small size of that effect seems incompatible with the "double trigger" hypothesis, in which financial distress plays a major role in the mortgage default decision. However, as documented by Gyourko and Tracy (2013), the finding of a weak correlation between unemployment rates and default is common in the literature. Those authors argue that the small estimated effect of unemployment on default probabilities is due to attenuation bias arising from the noisy relationship between unemployment rates and an individual borrower's employment status. Although Gyourko and Tracy explain the apparent disconnect between the results of studies that use data on individual borrowers' employment statuses and studies that use aggregate unemployment statistics, their work does not imply that default and prepayment models using aggregate unemployment statistics

Table 4.3: Quarterly Conditional Default and Prepayment Model
Panel A: Default

Explanatory Variable[1]	Coefficient[2]	Marginal Effect[3,4]	Explanatory Variable (cont'd.)	Coefficient[2]	Marginal Effect[3,4]
Constant	-9.04*	-	Loan Size Ratio≤30		
Age_t≤2[5]	1.16*	78.0%	30<Loan Size Ratio≤40	-0.04	-5.5%
2<Age_t≤4	0.14*	2.5%	40<Loan Size Ratio≤50	-0.10*	-13.0%
4<Age_t≤8	0.11*	4.8%	50<Loan Size Ratio≤60	-0.18*	-21.0%
8<Age_t≤12	0.03	-1.6%	60<Loan Size Ratio≤70	-0.25*	-29.0%
12<Age_t≤16	0.02	-1.2%	70<Loan Size Ratio≤80	-0.31*	-34.0%
16<Age_t≤20	0.00	-1.7%	Loan Size Ratio>80	-0.30*	-33.0%
20<Age_t≤36	0.01	-1.8%	LTV≤80		
Age_t>36	0.00	-0.9%	80<LTV≤90	0.12	15.0%
0≤PNEG≤0.025			90<LTV≤95	-0.04	-5.4%
0.025≤PNEG≤0.05	0.86*	43.0%	95<LTV≤97	-0.09	-11.0%
0.05≤PNEG≤0.1	1.14*	68.0%	LTV>97	-0.23*	-24.0%
0.1≤PNEG≤0.15	1.38*	95.0%	MP_t≤-6		
0.15≤PNEG≤0.2	1.54*	120.0%	-6<MP_t≤3	0.17*	12.0%
0.2≤PNEG≤0.3	1.70*	140.0%	3<MP_t≤9	0.37*	27.0%
0.3≤PNEG≤0.4	1.92*	190.0%	9<MP_t≤15	0.53*	41.0%
0.4≤PNEG≤0.5	2.02*	210.0%	15<MP_t≤20	0.71*	58.0%
0.5≤PNEG≤0.75	2.23*	260.0%	MP_t>20	1.04*	100.0%
PNEG≥0.75	2.67*	410.0%	Change in State Unemp. Rate	-0.10*	-9.2%
FICO≤499					
499<FICO≤559	-0.27*	-41.0%	Outside Downpayment Source	0.65*	64.0%
559<FICO≤599	-0.46*	-65.0%	Refinance	0.33*	32.0%
599<FICO≤639	-0.66*	-85.0%	FY ORIG < 1995	-0.90*	-
639<FICO≤659	-0.92*	-110.0%	FY ORIG < 2000	-0.31*	-
659<FICO≤679	-1.06*	-120.0%	First calendar quarter		
679<FICO≤719	-1.33*	-130.0%	Second calendar quarter	0.06*	5.2%
FICO>719	-1.88*	-150.0%	Third calendar quarter	0.11*	10.0%
FICO not available	-0.52*	-72.0%	Fourth calendar quarter	0.08*	7.9%
DTI<35					
35≤DTI<41	0.04*	3.8%			
DTI>41	0.05	4.2%			
DTI not available	0.17*	16.0%			

Notes:
1. See table 4.1 for a detailed description of each variable.
2. Coefficients are marked with an asterisk if they are statistically significant at the 5-percent confidence level, where standard errors were clustered by credit subsidy cohort.
3. Marginal effects for all variables except age are calculated fixing age at 20 quarters, origination year dummies at zero, and all other variables at their sample averages. Marginal effects for age are calculated holding other variables at values described above, but calculating the marginal effect for each portion of the age spline function.
4. Marginal effects are expressed as a proportion of the sample average probabilities of default and prepayment for a loan of age 20 quarters.
5. All of the variables are indicators except for the following: age is a linear spline function with knot points at the indicated values; change in state unemployment rate is a continuous variable.

Table 4.3: Quarterly Conditional Default and Prepayment Model
Panel B: Prepayment

Explanatory Variable[1]	Coefficient[2]	Marginal Effect[3,4]	Explanatory Variable (cont'd.)	Coefficient[2]	Marginal Effect[3,4]
Constant	-8.37*	-	Loan Size Ratio≤30		
Age_t≤2[5]	1.59*	45.0%	30<Loan Size Ratio≤40	0.26*	17.0%
2<Age_t≤4	0.26*	30.0%	40<Loan Size Ratio≤50	0.46*	32.0%
4<Age_t≤8	0.07	11.0%	50<Loan Size Ratio≤60	0.62*	47.0%
8<Age_t≤12	-0.02	0.7%	60<Loan Size Ratio≤70	0.75*	60.0%
12<Age_t≤16	-0.03	-0.1%	70<Loan Size Ratio≤80	0.83*	69.0%
16<Age_t≤20	-0.03	-0.5%	Loan Size Ratio>80	0.91*	80.0%
20<Age_t≤36	-0.01	1.0%	LTV≤80		
Age_t>36	-0.02*	-3.0%	80<LTV≤90	-0.08*	-6.5%
0≤PNEG≤0.025			90<LTV≤95	0.09*	7.9%
0.025≤PNEG≤0.05	-0.41*	-47.0%	95<LTV≤97	0.17*	15.0%
0.05≤PNEG≤0.1	-0.61*	-65.0%	LTV>97	0.17*	15.0%
0.1≤PNEG≤0.15	-0.76*	-77.0%	MP_t≤-6		
0.15≤PNEG≤0.2	-0.86*	-84.0%	-6<MP_t≤3	0.20*	8.3%
0.2≤PNEG≤0.3	-1.07*	-96.0%	3<MP_t≤9	0.60*	31.0%
0.3≤PNEG≤0.4	-1.31*	-110.0%	9<MP_t≤15	1.09*	72.0%
0.4≤PNEG≤0.5	-1.19*	-100.0%	15<MP_t≤20	1.52*	130.0%
0.5≤PNEG≤0.75	-0.85*	-84.0%	MP_t>20	1.74*	160.0%
PNEG≥0.75	-0.82*	-83.0%	Change in State Unemp. Rate	-0.04	-3.8%
FICO≤499					
499<FICO≤559	-0.02	-1.4%	Outside Downpayment Source	-0.20*	-19.0%
559<FICO≤599	0.16	12.0%	Refinance	0.16*	15.0%
599<FICO≤639	0.27*	21.0%	FY ORIG < 1995	-0.22*	-
639<FICO≤659	0.38*	32.0%	FY ORIG < 2000	-0.19*	-
659<FICO≤679	0.40*	33.0%	First calendar quarter		
679<FICO≤719	0.48*	41.0%	Second calendar quarter	0.20*	19.0%
FICO>719	0.54*	48.0%	Third calendar quarter	0.01	1.1%
FICO not available	0.36*	29.0%	Fourth calendar quarter	0.02	2.2%
DTI<35					
35≤DTI<41	0.08*	7.2%			
DTI>41	0.16*	15.0%			
DTI not available	-0.01	-0.8%			

Notes:

1. See table 4.1 for a detailed description of each variable.

2. Coefficients are marked with an asterisk if they are statistically significant at the 5-percent confidence level, where standard errors were clustered by credit subsidy cohort.

3. Marginal effects for all variables except age are calculated fixing age at 20 quarters, origination year dummies at zero, and all other variables at their sample averages. Marginal effects for age are calculated holding other variables at values described above, but calculating the marginal effect for each portion of the age spline function.

4. Marginal effects are expressed as a proportion of the sample average probabilities of default and prepayment for a loan of age 20 quarters.

5. All of the variables are indicators except for the following: age is a linear spline function with knot points at the indicated values; change in state unemployment rate is a continuous variable.

provide biased forecasts.[14] Because individual employment status is significantly less predictable than the overall unemployment rate, it would be difficult to ascertain whether a model that incorporated individual employment status would provide significantly more accurate forecasts of mortgage default and prepayment.

The results in this analysis for prepayment behavior are also broadly consistent with theory and previous research. The baseline probability of prepayment rises for the first twelve quarters of a loan's life and declines thereafter. A higher probability of negative equity tends to be associated with a lower probability of prepayment, consistent with the notion that negative equity in the home poses an obstacle to refinancing. The marginal effects imply that moving from a probability of negative equity in the 5 to 10 percent range to the 10 to 15 percent range reduces the probability of prepayment by roughly 11 percent. A higher borrower FICO score is associated with a higher probability of prepayment. Moving from a borrower FICO score in the range 659 to 679 to the range 679 to 719 increases the probability of prepayment by roughly 8 percent.

A higher loan-to-value ratio at origination is associated with a higher probability of prepayment. That relationship may reflect the idea that high LTV borrowers are likely to refinance into cheaper conventional mortgages once they have built equity in the home, whereas lower LTV borrowers have obtained FHA financing for reasons other than the lack of a large down payment. Moving from an original loan-to-value ratio in the 90 to 95 percent range to the 95 to 97 percent range is associated with a roughly 7 percent increase in the probability of prepayment.

Consistent with a financial option interpretation of prepayment behavior, loans with high mortgage premiums are more likely to be prepaid than loans with low or negative mortgage premiums. For instance, moving from a mortgage premium in the range of 9 to 15 percent to the range of 15 to 20 percent is associated with a 58 percent higher probability of prepayment. Larger mortgages have a higher probability of prepayment. Moving from a loan size ratio in the range of 50 to 60 percent to the range of 60 to 70 percent increases the probability of prepayment by 13 percent.

A higher debt-to-income ratio is associated with a higher probability of prepayment, with an increase in the debt-to-income ratio from the 0 to 35 percent range to the 35 to 41 percent range associated with a 7 percent higher probability of prepayment. Refinance status also increases the probability of prepayment by nearly 15 percent, while use of an outside down payment source decreases the probability of prepayment by 19 percent. Changes in the unemployment rate have a statistically insignificant effect on the probability of prepayment, with a one percentage point increase in the unemployment rate associated with a 4 percent decrease in prepayment probability. Loans originated prior to fiscal year 2000 exhibit lower prepayment probabilities than loans originated more recently, holding other characteristics constant.

---

[14] Several alternative specifications for unemployment were tested, including using functions of the level of the unemployment rate rather than its change and using a "homeowners-only" unemployment rate as suggested by Gyourko and Tracy. The results from those alternative specifications were similar to the results presented in this paper.

5. Loss Severity

After FHA pays a claim on a defaulted loan, the lender conveys the property to FHA, which then sells the property to defray its losses. The loss FHA incurs is the claim payment (the unpaid balance of the loan, UPB) minus the selling-price (V) net of costs associated with the foreclosure (c), including missed interest payments and selling fees. To facilitate comparison across different loan sizes, the loss given default (LGD) is expressed as a fraction of the unpaid balance:

$$LGD = \frac{UPB - V + c}{UPB}.$$

CBO models LGD as a linear function of loan characteristics and macroeconomic variables at the time of default,

$$LGD_{it} = \alpha + \beta X_{it} + \varepsilon_{it},$$

where X_{it} is a vector of loan i's characteristics at time t, β is a vector of the parameters to be estimated, and ε_{it} is a random error.

5.1 Data

The entire sample of loans that end in default is included in the analysis of loss given default; both the randomly selected loans and the over-sampled defaults from the original data set are included. The estimation sample is restricted to loans that defaulted between January 2000 and December 2009 because the data indicate that many claims associated with default events occurring later had not yet been fully resolved by the end of the data sample. The loan characteristics and economic variables used to model LGD are described in Table 5.1.

Table 5.2 presents descriptive statistics for selected variables. As in the default and prepayment model, the continuous variables are re-coded as categorical variables that take the value one if the variable is within a certain range and zero otherwise, while age enters as a linear spline function. Those transformations allow for the explanatory variables to have potentially nonlinear effects on loss given default.

Table 5.2 shows that a significant majority of loans that eventually default have original loan-to-value ratios greater than 97 percent. Eighty-eight percent of the loans that default are estimated to have a current loan-to-value ratio (CLTV) between 70 and 100 percent at the time of default based on the amortization of the mortgage and house price appreciation in their area. In reality, it is likely that many of those mortgages are actually underwater, with CLTVs greater than 100 percent, because FHA's property appraisals indicate that the median CLTV is 112 percent at the time of foreclosure. The discrepancy probably arises from the procedure for estimating CLTV, which uses the change in the house price index (HPI) for the entire Metropolitan Statistical Area (MSA) or, if not applicable, the state where the property is located; that approach neglects the dispersion of individual home prices around local trends. Loans that enter foreclosure are likely to have experienced lower than average price appreciation for their geographical area. However, the data set does not contain appraisal values for loans that do not default, which precludes using that measure in the simulation of future loan performance. Therefore, the less

Variable	Coding	Description
Loan-to-value ratio (LTV)	Categorical	The ratio of the original mortgage amount to the value of the mortgaged property at the time of loan origination.
Borrower credit score (FICO)	Categorical	The lowest decision score across borrowers on a loan application, where each borrower's credit score is the median of reported scores. Available after May 2004.
Loan size ratio	Categorical	The ratio of the original mortgage amount to the original amount of the average mortgage guaranteed by Fannie Mae or Freddie Mac originated in the same state and year.
Refinance	Indicator	An indicator for whether the loan is a purchase loan or a refinance. Refinance status does not depend on whether the original loan was an FHA loan.
Outside downpayment source	Indicator	An indicator for whether the borrower used an outside source of funds for the down payment.
Age	Spline	The age of the loan in quarters at the time of default. The linear spline function for age allows the loss given default to vary flexibly with the age of the loan.
Current loan-to-value ratio (CLTV)	Categorical	The ratio of the unpaid principal balance of the mortgage to the estimated market value of the property at the time of default.
House price appreciation rate (HPR)	Categorical	The rate of appreciation of the MSA-level house price index between two quarters prior to default and 4 quarters after default. The four quarters after default are included to account for the time-consuming nature of the foreclosure process.
State indicators	Indicator	A set of indicator variables for the state where the property is located. Controls for characteristics of the foreclosure process and other state-level variation in loss given default.

accurate measure—where CLTV is calculated using the change of the HPI—is used in the loss given default model.

Qi and Yang (2009) find that homes with higher-than-average value tend to have lower loss rates, which they attribute partially to the presence of costs of foreclosure, such as lawyers' fees, that do not scale up with home values. The loan size ratio is included to control for that effect. The average loan size ratio of loans that eventually default is smaller than the average loan size ratio for FHA loans overall, as suggested by the results in section 4.3.

Indicator variables for the state where the property is located are included in the model to account for differences in foreclosure processes and housing markets. Judicial characteristics that vary across states have been shown to have a large effect on the length of time a loan spends in foreclosure and on the willingness of a borrower to default. For a full discussion of the effects of state judicial characteristics, see Pence (2006) and Qi and Yang (2009).

Table 5.2: Descriptive Statistics for Loss Given Default Model

Variable	Sample Mean	Variable	Sample Mean
CLTV		*LTV*	
CLTV ≤ 60	4.0%	LTV ≤ 80	0.6%
60 < CLTV ≤ 70	8.3%	80 < LTV ≤ 90	5.3%
70 < CLTV ≤ 80	20.2%	90 < LTV ≤ 95	7.0%
80 < CLTV ≤ 90	37.5%	95 < LTV ≤ 97	36.0%
90 < CLTV ≤ 100	27.5%	LTV > 97	51.0%
100 < CLTV ≤ 110	1.5%		
110 < CLTV ≤ 120	0.5%	*FICO*	
CLTV > 120	0.4%	FICO ≤ 499	0.3%
		499 < FICO ≤ 559	2.4%
HPR		559 < FICO ≤ 599	3.5%
HPR ≤ -0.12	3.7%	599 < FICO ≤ 639	3.9%
-0.12 < HPR ≤ -0.08	2.1%	639 < FICO ≤ 659	1.4%
-0.08 < HPR ≤ -0.04	3.5%	659 < FICO ≤ 679	0.9%
-0.04 < HPR ≤ 0	7.7%	679 < FICO ≤ 719	0.8%
0 < HPR ≤ 0.04	16.1%	FICO > 719	0.5%
0.04 < HPR ≤ 0.08	36.8%	NO FICO[1]	86.3%
0.08 < HPR ≤ 0.12	15.9%		
0.12 < HPR ≤ 0.16	7.6%	*AGE*	
HPR > 0.16	6.6%	AGE AT DEFAULT	13.8
LOAN SIZE RATIO		*LOAN DETAILS*	
Loan Size Ratio≤30	11.0%	REFINANCE	9.2%
30<Loan Size Ratio≤40	17.9%	OUTSIDE DOWNPAYMENT	18.7%
40<Loan Size Ratio≤50	20.8%		
50<Loan Size Ratio≤60	18.8%		
60<Loan Size Ratio≤70	14.2%		
70<Loan Size Ratio≤80	9.1%		
Loan Size Ratio>80	8.2%		

Notes:

1. FHA did not collect FICO data prior to 2004.

5.2 Results

Table 5.3 displays the results of the linear regression of loss given default as a percentage of the amount owed on the explanatory factors. All of the explanatory variables except for age are expressed as categorical variables, and age is expressed as a piecewise linear spline function.

House price appreciation and loan size ratio explain much of the variation in loss given default. House price appreciation rate (HPR) has the largest effect. A loan with HPR in the highest category, greater than 16 percent, is predicted to have a loss rate 60 percentage points lower than a loan with HPR in the lowest category, less than negative 12 percent. Loans with lower origination values tend to have higher loss rates. Homes with a loan size ratio in the highest category, greater than 80, have loss rates that are 30 percentage points lower on average than homes with a loan size ratio less than 30.

As expected, the severity of loss is increasing in current LTV and decreasing in borrower FICO score. However, the estimates for FICO and CLTV indicate that those characteristics are less important for estimating loss given default than they are for estimating the probabilities of default and prepayment. Moving from the lowest CLTV category of less than 60 percent to the highest category of greater than 120 percent predicts just an 18 percentage point increase in the loss rate, while moving from the lowest FICO score category, below 499, to the highest category, above 719, predicts a decrease in the loss rate of only 10 percentage points. The relatively weak effect of CLTV on loss severity is likely to arise because the calculated CLTV is a noisy proxy for the true current LTV of the property. Noise in the calculated value for CLTV will attenuate its estimated effect on loss severity.

Loss severity increases as a loan matures, holding the other regressors constant. A possible explanation for that increase is that the fixed costs associated with foreclosure make up a larger portion of the loan balance when a loan has had more time to amortize. The spline function allows for nonlinear effects, but the estimated function is nearly linear. The indicator variables for the state in which the property is located have a large impact on loss given default estimates. Consistent with previous research, loss rates are higher in states that require a judicial foreclosure process. The state coefficients are omitted from Table 5.3 to conserve space.

6. Projections

CBO uses the statistical models of default and prepayment probabilities and loss given default to project the cash flows over the lifetime of FHA's current and future cohorts of guaranteed mortgages. Because many variables in the models depend on macroeconomic conditions, the projections rely on CBO's forecasts of several macroeconomic series. Additionally, projecting certain characteristics of FHA's recent and future cohorts of guarantees is necessary in order to project their subsequent performance. To generate a range of possible outcomes for FHA's portfolio of loan guarantees, CBO simulates 1,000 paths for the macroeconomic variables, and samples from the estimated distribution of parameters in the statistical model of mortgage default and prepayment to account for the uncertainty in those estimated parameters.

Table 5.3: Loss Given Default Model

Variable[1]	Coefficient	Variable (continued)	Coefficient
0 < AGE ≤ 3	-0.026	Loan Size Ratio≤30	
3 < AGE ≤ 7	-0.004	30<Loan Size Ratio≤40	0.163
7 < AGE ≤ 11	0.002	40<Loan Size Ratio≤50	-0.110
11 < AGE ≤ 15	0.002	50<Loan Size Ratio≤60	-0.168
15 < AGE ≤ 19	0.003	60<Loan Size Ratio≤70	-0.213
19 < AGE ≤ 23	0.005	70<Loan Size Ratio≤80	-0.254
23 < AGE ≤ 27	0.003	Loan Size Ratio>80	-0.303
27 < AGE ≤ 31	0.008	LTV ≤ 80	
31 < AGE ≤ 35	0.001	80 < LTV ≤ 90	0.026
35 < AGE ≤ 39	0.003	90 < LTV ≤ 95	0.038
AGE > 39	0.005	95 < LTV ≤ 97	0.051
CLTV ≤ 60		LTV > 97	0.041
60 < CLTV ≤ 70	0.012	FICO ≤ 499	
70 < CLTV ≤ 80	0.050	499 < FICO ≤ 559	-0.034
80 < CLTV ≤ 90	0.087	559 < FICO ≤ 599	-0.056
90 < CLTV ≤ 100	0.105	599 < FICO ≤ 639	-0.075
100 < CLTV ≤ 110	0.090	639 < FICO ≤ 659	-0.089
110 < CLTV ≤ 120	0.121	659 < FICO ≤ 679	-0.095
CLTV > 120	0.175	679 < FICO ≤ 719	-0.101
HPR ≤ -0.12		FICO > 719	-0.104
-0.12 < HPR ≤ -0.08	-0.103	No FICO	-0.057
-0.08 < HPR ≤ -0.04	-0.142	Refinance	0.059
-0.04 < HPR ≤ 0	-0.212	Outside Downpayment	0.069
0 < HPR ≤ 0.04	-0.301		
0.04 < HPR ≤ 0.08	-0.382	State Dummies[2]	Yes
0.08 < HPR ≤ 0.12	-0.443		
0.12 < HPR ≤ 0.16	-0.509	Constant	0.768
HPR > 0.16	-0.600		
N	428,977	R-squared	0.424

Notes:

1. See table 5.1 for a detailed description of each variable. All of the explanatory variables except for age are expressed as categorical variables. Age is expressed as a piecewise linear spline function.

2. Estimates of coefficients on state dummies are omitted to preserve space.

6.1 Characteristics of Recent and Future Cohorts of Guarantees

The data set contains information on loans through the 2010 cohort. FHA reports summary statistics on the 2011 through 2013 cohorts in its quarterly reports to the Congress.[15] The data set and summary statistics for more recent years are used to simulate the loan level characteristics for FHA's 2011 through 2015 cohorts. The key simulated characteristics are the loan-to-value ratio at origination, the borrower FICO score, the loan size ratio, the spread between the mortgage interest rate and the 10-year Treasury rate, and the debt-to-income ratio.

In CBO's analysis, the projected geographic distribution of mortgage guarantees in the 2011 through 2015 cohorts matches its average from 2007 to 2010. The 2009 and 2010 cohorts, the most recent for which CBO has detailed data, form the basis for projecting the other loan characteristics of the 2011 through 2015 cohorts; CBO adjusts those characteristics to reflect changes in the reported composition of FHA's loan guarantees since 2010. The borrower's FICO score, the interest rate spread, the debt-to-income ratio, and the log loan size ratio are approximately normally distributed. Those variables are simulated using a multivariate normal distribution with parameters estimated using data from the 2009 and 2010 cohorts. Because the loan-to-value ratio is not normally distributed, it is simulated using a semiparametric approach in order to emulate its distribution and correlations with the other variables. All loan characteristics are simulated separately for refinances and purchase loans to match the distributions within the two groups. The refinance share for 2011 through 2013 is taken from historical data, and the share for 2014 through 2015 is selected to be consistent with historical trends and CBO's projections for the housing market. A distinction is made between streamline and fully underwritten refinances to account for their different fee structures and loan characteristics. The distribution of purchase loans and streamline and fully underwritten refinances is shown in Figure 6.1.

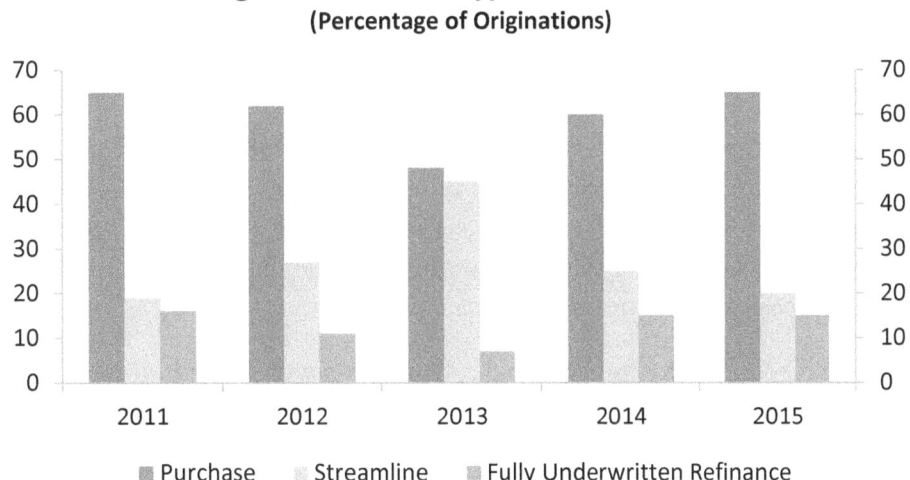

Figure 6.1: Loan Type Distribution
(Percentage of Originations)

---

[15] See Department of Housing and Urban Development (various years).

Further adjustments are made to the estimated characteristics of the 2014 and 2015 cohorts to account for the possibility that some borrowers will obtain other sources of financing in response to FHA's recent fee increases. The adjustments include reducing the volume-share of the loans with the smallest fair-value subsidies (as discussed in Section 7.2). Those reductions reflect the potential for adverse selection among those groups of borrowers, which have higher average FICO scores and lower credit risk. The adverse selection effect is projected to be larger for the 2015 cohort.

As noted in Section 4.2, FHA's streamline refinance loans were excluded from the statistical analysis because the corresponding loan records generally do not include loan-to-value ratios or borrower FICO scores. Thus, in CBO's main analysis, streamline refinance loans were modeled as exhibiting loan behavior similar to nonstreamline refinances in the same cohorts. However, as argued by Aragon and others (2010) and Caplin and others (2012), streamline refinances are likely to have higher loan-to-value ratios than nonstreamline refinances in the same cohort, and streamline refinance borrowers may potentially have lower FICO scores as well. Although those differences would likely lead to higher claim rates on streamline refinances, there are other differences between streamline refinances and nonstreamline refinances that would likely lead to offsetting effects on the cost of those loans. Most importantly, a higher loan-to-value ratio predicts lower prepayment rates, which will increase FHA's fee income. In addition, streamline refinance borrowers cannot take out cash at closing, and streamline refinances must provide a "net tangible benefit" to the borrower, currently defined in most cases as a minimum 5 percent reduction in the principal and interest plus mortgage insurance premium payments. Those lower payments should lead to lower claim rates because the streamline refinance mortgage is more affordable than the original mortgage, which need not be the case with nonstreamline refinances.

To assess the relative strength of the competing effects described above, CBO conducted tests of the model in which it compared the model's predicted default and claim rates for streamline refinances to the historical performance for those loans (additional detail is provided in the Appendix). Those tests indicate that claim rates predicted by the model were somewhat lower than in the data for the more recent cohorts (consistent with the modeling of Aragon and others and Caplin and others) but that prepayment rates predicted by the model were significantly higher than in the data for those cohorts. The net impact of those differences was to increase costs in some cases but to decrease costs in other cases.

On the basis of those tests, CBO did not see evidence that costs were sufficiently higher or lower than estimated to warrant adjustment. (CBO reports the sensitivity of costs to alternative values for the distribution of initial loan-to-value ratios of streamline refinances in the appendix.) CBO will revisit that modeling issue in the future because data that CBO has recently acquired from FHA will allow for better inferences about the characteristics of streamline refinances.

Figure 6.2 shows selected statistics for the simulated cohorts along with recent history. However, FHA's actual cohorts of loan guarantees could differ from CBO's projections in a number of ways. The Appendix examines the sensitivity of the results to the composition of the 2014 and 2015 cohorts. CBO projects that FHA will guarantee $150 billion in new mortgages in each of the 2014 and 2015 cohorts. CBO has not attempted to quantify the effect on the estimated subsidies of the uncertainty associated with the volume of guarantees in those cohorts.

Figure 6.2: Loan Characteristics by Cohort

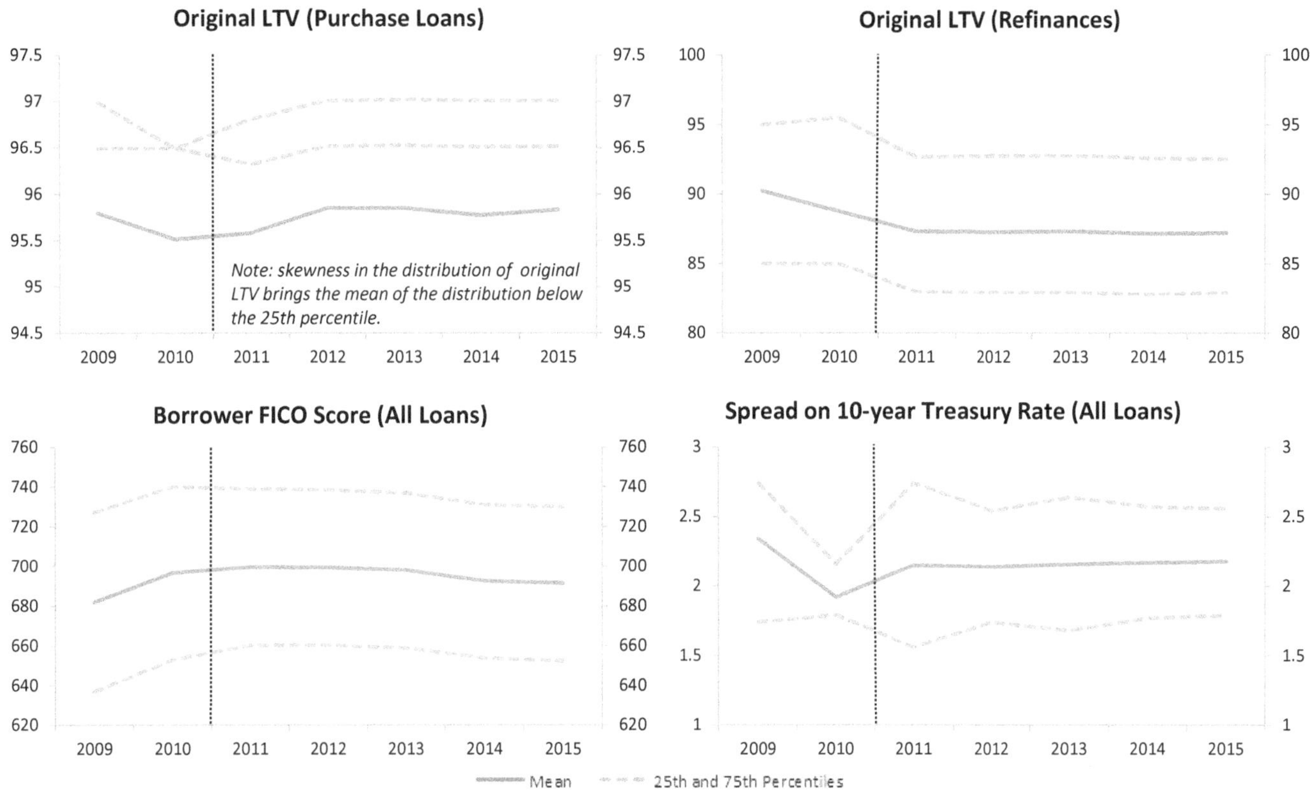
Original LTV (Purchase Loans)
97.5
97
96.5
96
95.5
95
94.5
2009 2010 2011 2012 2013 2014 2015
Note: skewness in the distribution of original LTV brings the mean of the distribution below the 25th percentile.
Original LTV (Refinances)
100
95
90
85
80
2009 2010 2011 2012 2013 2014 2015
Borrower FICO Score (All Loans)
760
740
720
700
680
660
640
620
2009 2010 2011 2012 2013 2014 2015
Spread on 10-year Treasury Rate (All Loans)
3
2.5
2
1.5
1
2009 2010 2011 2012 2013 2014 2015
Mean
25th and 75th Percentiles

Note: vertical lines represent end of CBO's data sample.

6.2 Macroeconomic Conditions

CBO simulates multiple paths for several macroeconomic variables so that the mean of each series matches the baseline forecast for 2014 to 2024 described by CBO (2014a). The baseline paths use a smooth five year transition for the variables from their values as of the end of 2024 to their long-run values as given by CBO (2013a). The agency has since released updated economic projections. The key macroeconomic variables interest rates, house prices, and the unemployment rate. CBO (2013a) does not project house prices in its long-term outlook; in this analysis, the estimates are based on national house price appreciation of 3 percent per year after 2024.

One thousand paths of the one- and ten-year Treasury rates were simulated using the two-factor version of the model devised by Cox, Ingersoll, and Ross (1985). The 30-year mortgage rate is simulated by adding a constant spread to the simulated levels of the 10-year Treasury rate. CBO also simulated one thousand paths for national house prices by appending eight-quarter periods of national house price appreciation chosen randomly from data for the second quarter of 1971 through the third quarter of 2013. That process is meant to mimic the persistence in house price changes observed in the data. The unemployment rate is simulated by regressing historical unemployment on its one-quarter lagged value, the one and ten year Treasury rates, and the quarterly change in house prices. Then for each simulated path of interest rates and house prices, CBO computed the unemployment rate predicted by that regression and added a random

Figure 6.3: Macroeconomic Simulations

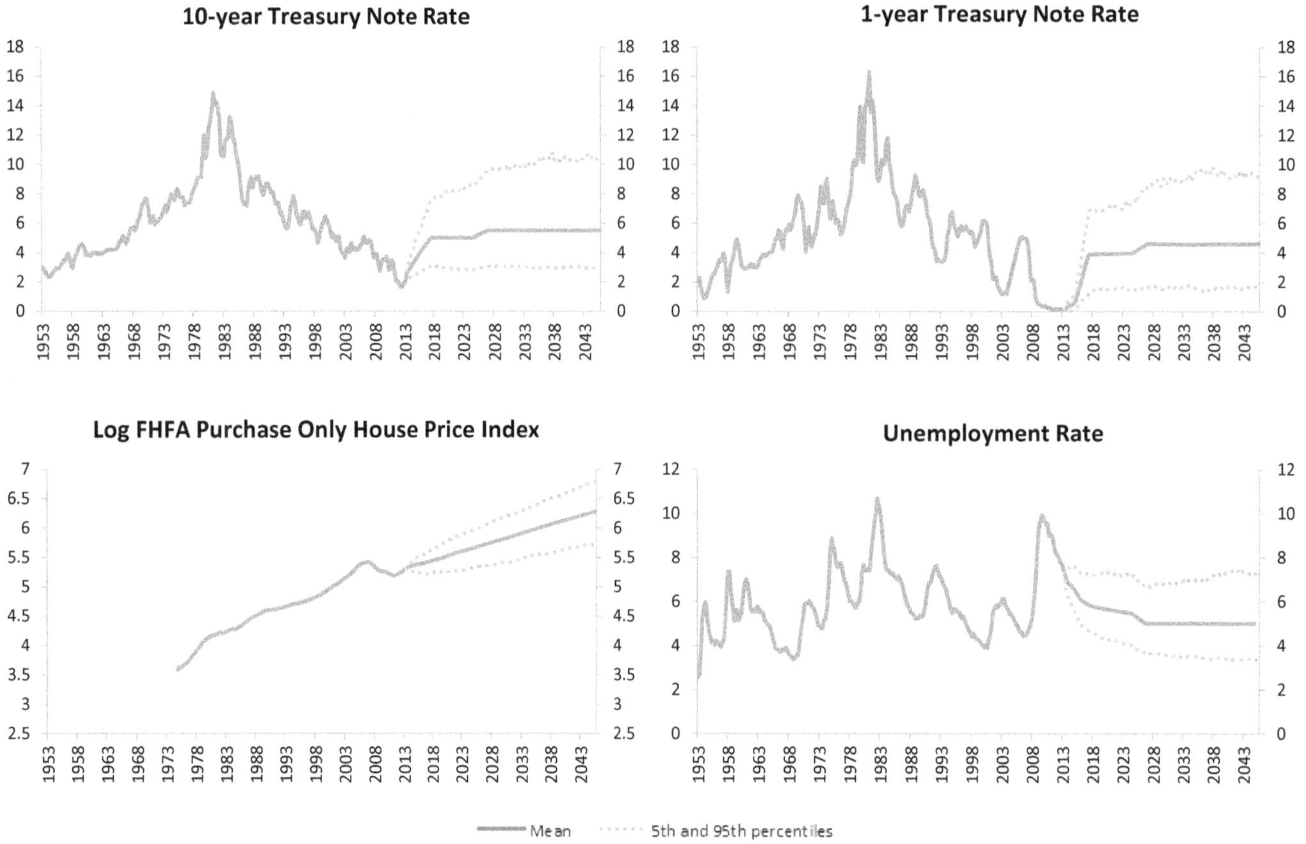

10-year Treasury Note Rate

1-year Treasury Note Rate

Log FHFA Purchase Only House Price Index

Unemployment Rate

Mean .... 5th and 95th percentiles

Note: Projections shown for fiscal years 2014 to 2045. FHFA Purchase Only House Price Index extrapolated to grow at 3 percent annually from fiscal year 2024 to 2045. FHFA Purchase Only House Price Index is backcasted prior to 1991 using the Freddie Mac Conventional Mortgage Home Price Index.

error. The series were then rescaled to have average values that are consistent with CBO's economic projections. Figure 6.3 illustrates the 5th to 95th percentile ranges of the simulated paths for the macroeconomic variables.

6.3 Results

CBO simulated the performance of the 1992 through 2015 cohorts of FHA mortgage guarantees through their maturity dates using each of the 1,000 simulations of macroeconomic conditions. The estimated models for default, prepayment, and loss given default provide projected outcomes for the cohorts at a quarterly frequency. Loan behavior, however, is not simulated at the individual loan level. Instead, loans are aggregated into small groups with similar characteristics, which greatly reduces the computational burden of the simulation process.[16]

CBO introduces two sources of uncertainty into the simulation results in addition to the variation in macroeconomic conditions. First, the model allows for uncertainty in the estimated parameters in the

---

[16] CBO conducted a preliminary analysis at the loan level, which produced similar results to the analysis with loans aggregated in small groups.

prepayment and default equations but not in the loss given default equation. Instead of using the point estimates for the parameters in each simulation path, each path uses parameters drawn randomly from the distribution implied by the statistical model, using standard errors for the parameters clustered at the cohort level. That process reflects the uncertainty inherent in the estimated statistical model. The sampling process has a small effect on the central outcomes for each cohort but increases the dispersion around those central outcomes compared to using fixed parameters. Second, random errors are added to the predicted prepayment and default probabilities from the model. The distribution of those errors is chosen to match the distribution of the errors in the model's predicted prepayment and default probabilities over history relative to actual experience. CBO's statistical model predicts the timing of mortgage default, that is, when a borrower enters 90-day delinquency prior to a claim eventually occurring. CBO models the delay between default and claim to approximate the observed distribution in the dataset between 2000 and 2009.

Figure 6.4 shows the claim, prepayment, and loss given default rates across the simulations. The averages represent CBO's expectation for the performance of the cohorts. The figure also displays the 5th and 95th percentiles of the values in the simulations. The numbers underlying Figure 6.4 are presented in Table A.1.

Figure 6.4 illustrates the sharp deterioration and then improvement in the performance of the cohorts since 2002. The 2002 cohort is estimated to have a cumulative lifetime claim rate of roughly 9 percent, about in line with the average for the 1992 through 1999 cohorts. In contrast, the 2006 and 2007 cohorts are projected to have cumulative lifetime claim rates of roughly 30 percent, reflecting the steep decline in house prices that began shortly after those loans were guaranteed. However, with the gradual improvement in economic conditions and the tightening of FHA's underwriting standards, the 2011 through 2015 cohorts have much lower expected lifetime claim rates, ranging from roughly 5 percent to roughly 8 percent. Similarly, estimated lifetime prepayment rates fall from roughly 90 percent for the 1990s and early 2000s cohorts to 61 percent for the 2006 cohort and then nearly return to their prerecession levels for the 2011 and later cohorts. Estimated loss given default rates rose because the decline in house prices reduced the amount of equity borrowers had in their homes. Then they fall to be roughly the same for the 2011 through 2015 cohorts as for the cohorts in the 1990s, owing to expectations of rising house prices.

In 90 percent of model simulations, the lifetime claim rate for the 2013 cohort is between 2.3 and 14.4 percent and the lifetime prepayment rate is between 68.3 and 94.2 percent. There is less uncertainty about the lifetime performance of older cohorts of loans because a lower proportion of those loans remains in place and older loans exhibit lower conditional probabilities of prepayment and default.

The percentiles of the projections illustrate the degree of uncertainty about default and prepayment behavior arising from the sources of variation that CBO models. Actual default and prepayment behavior may be more variable than implied by the model for a number of reasons:

- The statistical models of mortgage prepayment, default, and loss given default may be misspecified;
- Macroeconomic circumstances may develop in a way not captured by the model simulations; or

Figure 6.4: Simulated Lifetime Loan Performance by Cohort

Claim Rate

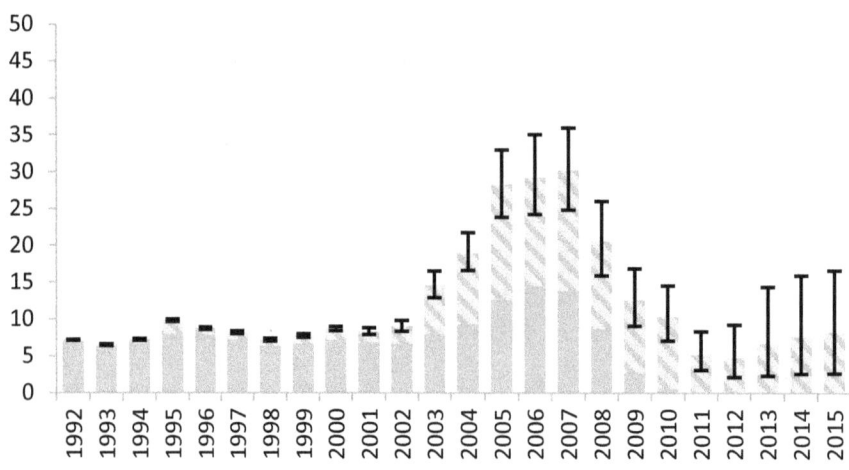

Prepayment Rate

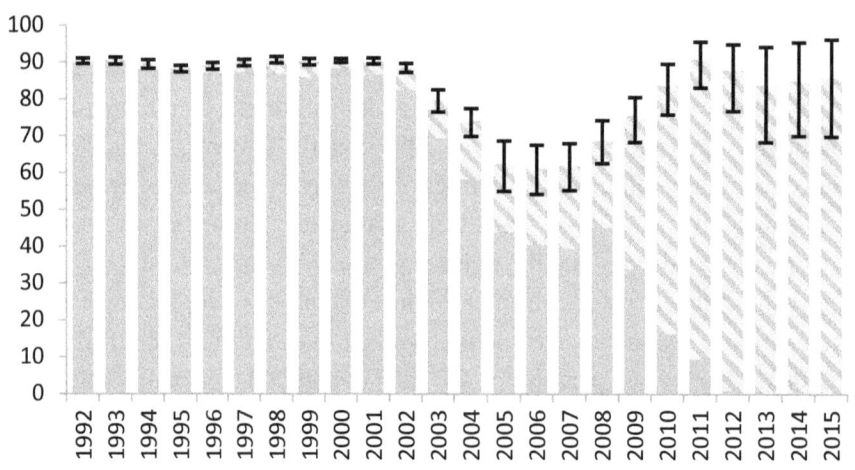

Loss Given Default

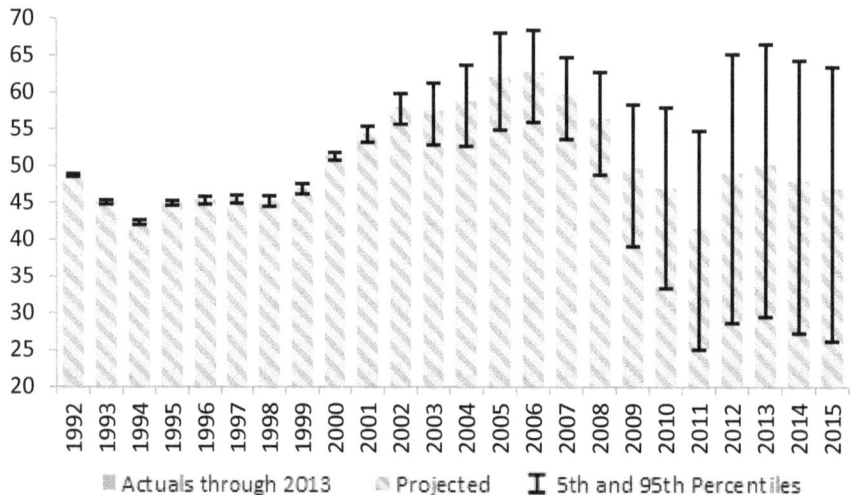

▓ Actuals through 2013   ▨ Projected   I 5th and 95th Percentiles

Note: Actuals through 2013 from Department of Housing and Urban Development (2013a).

- The characteristics of FHA's future cohorts could be substantially different than CBO anticipates. (The appendix presents estimates of the subsidy rates under different projections of the composition of future cohorts.)

In addition, CBO's projections are based on current law, which may change in ways that materially affect the outcomes.

7. Subsidy Rates

To estimate subsidy rates for FHA's mortgage guarantees, CBO uses its projections of the lifetime behavior of the mortgages to project the program's cash inflows and outflows. The cash flows are then discounted to the time of loan disbursement so that a net present value and associated subsidy rate can be assigned to each cohort. In this study, CBO calculated subsidy rates both on a FCRA basis and, for cash flows after fiscal year 2013, on a fair-value basis. Because the fair-value subsidy rates include a charge for the cost of risk, they are substantially higher than the FCRA subsidy rates, by an average of 6.2 percent of original loan volume for the 2014 and 2015 cohorts. Comparing subsidy rates by loan-to-value ratio and borrower credit score reveals a pattern of cross-subsidization among FHA borrowers, with less risky borrowers subsidizing riskier ones. For example, borrowers with FICO scores of 720 or higher have fair-value subsidy rates more than 2 percentage points lower than borrowers with FICO scores between 560 and 600. CBO treats refinances of previously FHA-insured mortgages as new originations in the cohort in which the refinancing occurs. Other authors have discussed alternative approaches to accounting for those refinances.

7.1 FCRA Subsidy Rates
CBO accounts for the budgetary effects of FHA mortgage insurance following the procedures prescribed in the Federal Credit Reform Act of 1990 (FCRA). The act stipulates that accounting for federal discretionary credit programs must be done on an accrual basis, with projected cash flows discounted using interest rates on Treasury securities of comparable maturity. The subsidy cost to the government of FHA's loan guarantees is the net present value of estimated claim payments net of recoveries and fees at the time of loan disbursement. Therefore, the analysis of the 2013 and earlier cohorts considers cash flows that have already been realized and cash flows that CBO projects to occur in the future, all discounted to the time of loan disbursement. The already-realized cash flows are taken from the model rather than from FHA's reported results.

Figure 7.1 and Tables 7.1 and 7.2 show the estimates of FCRA subsidy rates in percentage terms and dollar terms, respectively, for FHA's 1992 through 2015 cohorts. CBO's estimates imply that the 1992 through 1999 and the 2011 through 2015 cohorts will generate net savings for the government on a FCRA basis and the 2000 through 2010 cohorts will generate net costs. The worse performance of the 2000 through 2010 cohorts than earlier and more recent cohorts can be attributed partly to lower fees and the poor macroeconomic performance during and since the recent recession. The 2005 through 2008 cohorts exhibit particularly poor performance according to those estimates, with subsidy rates between 6 percent and 10 percent and a total subsidy cost of $25 billion. CBO's estimate of the volume-weighted subsidy rate for the 1992 to 2015 period as a whole is negative 0.5 percent, which corresponds to a cost savings of

Figure 7.1: Estimated FCRA Subsidy Rates

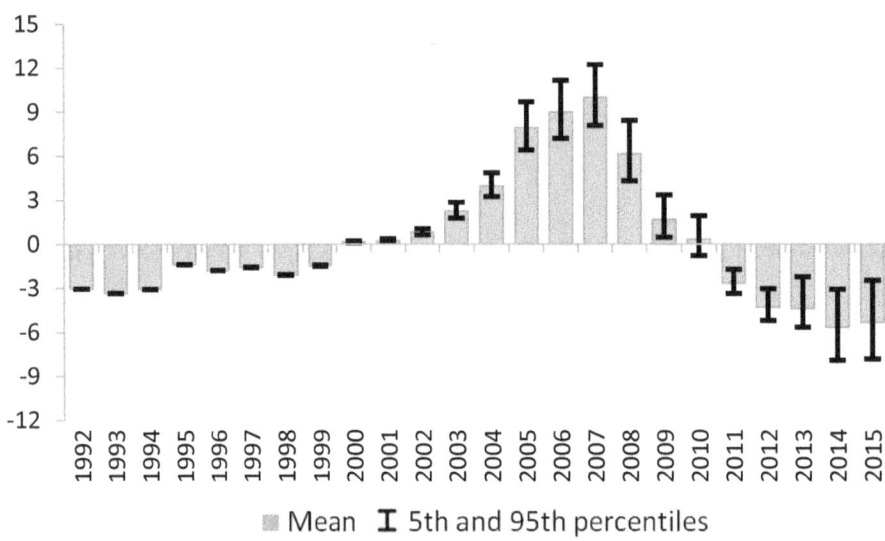

Mean I 5th and 95th percentiles

$14 billion. That estimate is similar to the rate implied by OMB's estimates for the same period, which is negative 0.7 percent.

Figure 7.1 and Tables 7.1 and 7.2 also provide information on the distribution of potential FCRA subsidy rates, showing the 5th and 95th percentiles of projected subsidy rates for each cohort. Larger proportions of loans from the later cohorts remain active, so if other factors were equal, more uncertainty would remain about the final performance of those cohorts. However, higher projected lifetime claim rates are associated with more uncertain subsidy rates. As a result, the 2005 through 2009 cohorts, which are projected to have high lifetime claim rates, have more uncertain subsidy rates than the 2010 through 2012 cohorts, which are projected to have lower lifetime claim rates.

In CBO's simulations, the 5th percentile of the total FCRA subsidy costs for the 1992 through 2015 cohorts is negative $43.2 billion, which corresponds to a weighted-average subsidy rate of negative 1.4 percent. The 95th percentile of those costs is positive $24 billion, which corresponds to a subsidy rate of 0.8 percent. Two-thirds of the simulated outcomes were between a subsidy cost for those loan guarantees of $3.4 billion (a subsidy rate of 0.1 percent) and a savings of $32.9 billion (a subsidy rate of negative 1.1 percent). The 1992 to 2013 cohorts, which have already been originated, are expected to have a FCRA subsidy cost of $2.2 billion (corresponding to a subsidy rate of 0.1 percent). The 5th percentile of the total subsidy costs for those cohorts is negative $19.6 billion (a subsidy rate of negative 0.7 percent), while the 95th percentile is positive $32.1 billion (a subsidy rate of 1.2 percent). In contrast, the 2014 and 2015 cohorts are expected to result in a FCRA subsidy cost of negative $16.4 billion (a subsidy rate of negative 5.5 percent), with a 5th percentile of negative $23.7 billion (a subsidy rate of negative 7.9 percent) and a 95th percentile of negative $8.3 billion (a subsidy rate of negative 2.8 percent). Therefore, those cohorts are quite unlikely to result in a positive FCRA subsidy cost, CBO estimates.

Table 7.1: Originated Volume and Estimated FCRA Subsidy Rates

Cohort	Volume ($ Billions)[1]	Subsidy Rate				
		Mean	5th Percentile[2]	17th Percentile[2]	83rd Percentile[2]	95th Percentile[2]
1992	43.4	-3.0%	-3.0%	-3.0%	-3.0%	-3.0%
1993	71.6	-3.3%	-3.3%	-3.3%	-3.3%	-3.3%
1994	82.4	-3.1%	-3.1%	-3.1%	-3.1%	-3.1%
1995	41.0	-1.4%	-1.4%	-1.4%	-1.4%	-1.4%
1996	64.2	-1.8%	-1.8%	-1.8%	-1.8%	-1.8%
1997	67.0	-1.6%	-1.6%	-1.6%	-1.6%	-1.6%
1998	93.3	-2.1%	-2.1%	-2.1%	-2.1%	-2.1%
1999	111.8	-1.5%	-1.5%	-1.5%	-1.4%	-1.4%
2000	84.9	0.1%	0.1%	0.1%	0.2%	0.2%
2001	121.6	0.2%	0.1%	0.2%	0.3%	0.4%
2002	131.4	0.8%	0.6%	0.7%	0.9%	1.0%
2003	116.0	2.3%	1.8%	1.9%	2.6%	2.9%
2004	107.6	4.0%	3.3%	3.5%	4.4%	4.9%
2005	58.0	7.9%	6.4%	6.9%	8.8%	9.7%
2006	51.8	9.0%	7.2%	7.8%	10.2%	11.2%
2007	56.5	10.0%	8.1%	8.8%	11.2%	12.2%
2008	171.8	6.2%	4.3%	5.0%	7.3%	8.4%
2009	330.5	1.7%	0.5%	0.9%	2.4%	3.4%
2010	297.6	0.3%	-0.8%	-0.4%	1.0%	1.9%
2011	217.7	-2.7%	-3.4%	-3.1%	-2.3%	-1.7%
2012	213.2	-4.3%	-5.2%	-4.9%	-3.8%	-3.0%
2013	240.0	-4.4%	-5.7%	-5.2%	-3.7%	-2.2%
Subtotal: Historical Cohorts	2773.2	0.1%	-0.7%	-0.4%	0.6%	1.2%
2014	150.0	-5.7%	-7.9%	-7.0%	-4.2%	-3.1%
2015	149.7	-5.3%	-7.9%	-7.0%	-3.8%	-2.5%
Subtotal: Future Cohorts	299.7	-5.5%	-7.9%	-7.0%	-4.0%	-2.8%
Total	3072.9	-0.5%	-1.4%	-1.1%	0.1%	0.8%

Notes:

1. Volume numbers for 1992 to 2012 are from the 2014 Federal Credit Supplement; volume numbers for 2013 through 2015 are CBO projections.

2. Percentiles are taken from 1,000 simulation paths described in section 6.

Table 7.2: Estimated FCRA Subsidies ($ Billions)

Cohort	Volume	Mean	5th Percentile[1]	17th Percentile[1]	83rd Percentile[1]	95th Percentile[1]
1992	43.4	-1.3	-1.3	-1.3	-1.3	-1.3
1993	71.6	-2.4	-2.4	-2.4	-2.4	-2.4
1994	82.4	-2.5	-2.5	-2.5	-2.5	-2.5
1995	41.0	-0.6	-0.6	-0.6	-0.6	-0.6
1996	64.2	-1.1	-1.2	-1.2	-1.1	-1.1
1997	67.0	-1.1	-1.1	-1.1	-1.0	-1.0
1998	93.3	-2.0	-2.0	-2.0	-1.9	-1.9
1999	111.8	-1.6	-1.7	-1.7	-1.6	-1.6
2000	84.9	0.1	0.1	0.1	0.1	0.2
2001	121.6	0.3	0.2	0.2	0.4	0.4
2002	131.4	1.1	0.8	0.9	1.2	1.4
2003	116.0	2.6	2.0	2.3	3.0	3.3
2004	107.6	4.3	3.5	3.8	4.8	5.2
2005	58.0	4.6	3.7	4.0	5.1	5.6
2006	51.8	4.7	3.7	4.0	5.3	5.8
2007	56.5	5.7	4.6	5.0	6.4	6.9
2008	171.8	10.6	7.4	8.6	12.5	14.5
2009	330.5	5.5	1.5	2.9	8.0	11.1
2010	297.6	0.9	-2.4	-1.2	3.1	5.8
2011	217.7	-5.8	-7.3	-6.8	-4.9	-3.8
2012	213.2	-9.2	-11.1	-10.4	-8.1	-6.5
2013	240.0	-10.5	-13.6	-12.5	-8.9	-5.4
Subtotal: Historical Cohorts	2773.2	2.2	-19.6	-11.9	15.4	32.1
2014	150.0	-8.5	-11.9	-10.6	-6.3	-4.6
2015	149.7	-8.0	-11.8	-10.5	-5.7	-3.7
Subtotal: Future Cohorts	299.7	-16.4	-23.7	-21.1	-12.0	-8.3
Total	3072.9	-14.3	-43.2	-32.9	3.4	23.8

Notes:

1. Percentiles are taken from 1,000 simulation paths described in section 6.

Table 7.3 shows how the range of estimated subsidy rates in the model simulations translates into a range capital reserve balances as of the end of fiscal year 2013, and compares those balances the values implied by the original and reestimated subsidy rates reported in the *Fiscal Year 2015 Federal Credit Supplement*. For each cohort, the estimated subsidy rates are converted to year-end fiscal 2013 values by multiplying by the dollar volume of the cohort and accumulating interest at the one-year Treasury rate as in Table 2.1.

The balance implied by the reestimated credit subsidy rates is negative $1.0 billion after accounting for the $4.3 billion transfer to the HECM financing account at the end of fiscal year 2013. That amount is nearly identical to what is reported in the most recent *Fiscal Year 2015 Federal Credit Supplement* and $73 billion less than would have been implied by the subsidy rates originally recorded in the budget. The mean subsidy rates estimated by CBO produce a balance of negative $1.2 billion (after accounting for the transfer to the HECM financing account), which is close to the value implied by the reestimated credit subsidy rates.

Using the 5th percentile of estimated subsidy rates produces a balance of positive $21.5 billion, while using the 95th percentile produces a balance of negative $32.2 billion (again, after accounting for the HECM transfer). Therefore, the 95th percentile outcome is associated with a $31 billion smaller balance as of the end of fiscal year 2013 than the mean outcome and the 5th percentile outcome is associated with a $23 billion larger balance than the mean outcome. The relatively narrow range of outcomes produced by the model relative to the size of the historical revisions in the estimated subsidy rates stems partially from the fact that much of the uncertainty concerning the older cohorts has already been resolved.

The balance of the capital reserve implied by the simulations does not correspond to the amount that FHA would need to draw from the Treasury in various scenarios. Indeed, the model implies that the 2014 and 2015 cohorts will result in substantial savings on a FCRA basis, which should substantially improve the status of FHA's capital reserves.

7.2 Fair-Value Subsidy Rates

CBO's fair-value estimates represent the estimated compensation that a private investor in an orderly market would require to assume FHA's obligations and fee income for the 1992 to 2015 cohorts. CBO estimates the fair-value subsidy as the estimated fair value of claims arising from FHA's loan guarantees minus the estimated fair value of FHA's fee income from those loan guarantees. The fair value of the claims arising from the loan guarantees is calculated as the difference in present value between the cash flows associated with loans that are fully guaranteed against default risk and the cash flows associated with loans that lack such a guarantee. That calculation follows from standard financial valuation principles (see, for example, Chapter 24 of Brealey and others (2006)). By providing a guarantee, the guarantor is effectively converting a loan with default risk into one without default risk, so the value of that insurance is the difference between the values of the guaranteed and nonguaranteed loans. Because the guaranteed and nonguaranteed loans have different risk profiles, their associated cash flows are discounted at different rates. Thus, the fair-value subsidy comprises three components: the value of a guaranteed loan, the value of a nonguaranteed loan, and the value of the fee income.

CBO estimates that the total fair-value subsidy cost associated with FHA's outstanding and projected portfolio of loan guarantees for the 1992 to 2015 cohorts is $65.4 billion. That estimate corresponds to the compensation that a private investor in an orderly market would be expected to require in order to assume FHA's remaining financial liabilities and fee income associated with those cohorts.

Table 7.3: Alternative Estimates of the Balance of FHA's MMIF[1]
End of Fiscal Year 2013

Cohort	Total Contribution to Capital Reserve Account Implied by:				
	FCS Original Estimate[2] ($ bil.)	FCS Reestimate[2] ($ bil.)	CBO Mean ($ bil.)	CBO 5th Percentile[3] ($ bil.)	CBO 95th Percentile[3] ($ bil.)
1992	2.2	2.8	2.6	2.6	2.6
1993	3.7	3.6	4.5	4.6	4.5
1994	4.2	2.7	4.6	4.7	4.6
1995	1.4	0.5	1.0	1.0	1.0
1996	2.9	1.1	1.9	1.9	1.9
1997	3.0	1.1	1.6	1.7	1.6
1998	4.1	2.0	2.9	2.9	2.9
1999	4.1	2.0	2.3	2.4	2.2
2000	2.3	-0.3	-0.2	-0.1	-0.2
2001	3.3	-0.2	-0.4	-0.2	-0.6
2002	3.3	-0.8	-1.3	-1.0	-1.7
2003	3.5	-1.7	-3.2	-2.5	-4.0
2004	3.2	-3.5	-5.1	-4.2	-6.2
2005	1.2	-5.5	-5.3	-4.3	-6.5
2006	1.0	-4.9	-5.2	-4.2	-6.5
2007	0.2	-7.2	-6.0	-4.9	-7.4
2008	0.4	-14.7	-10.9	-7.6	-14.9
2009	0.2	-6.8	-5.5	-1.5	-11.2
2010	2.6	1.5	-1.0	2.4	-5.8
2011	6.8	6.8	5.8	7.4	3.8
2012	5.4	10.4	9.2	11.1	6.5
2013	17.4	14.5	10.6	13.6	5.4
Subtotal: Excluding Transfer to HECM Financing Account	76.4	3.3	3.1	25.7	-28.0
Transfer to HECM Financing Account	-4.3	-4.3	-4.3	-4.3	-4.3
Total	72.2	-1.0	-1.2	21.5	-32.2

1. The calculations exclude the contributions of the HECM guarantees except for the FY 2013 transfer to the HECM financing account.
2. FCS refers to the 2015 Federal Credit Supplement, which reports both original and reestimated subsidy rates.
3. Percentiles are taken from 1,000 random simulation paths described in section 6. The simulations reflect uncertainty in estimated model parameters and future macroeconomic conditions. They do not reflect several other potentially important sources of uncertainty, such as possible policy changes at FHA or in the broader housing market, or variation in the composition of future cohorts.

Valuing Guaranteed Loans. To determine the value of a guaranteed loan, the cash flows associated with that loan are discounted to the present using a discount rate equal to the Treasury note rate of comparable maturity to the loan plus a spread that reflects the compensation that investors demand to bear the prepayment risk associated with the loan, called the option adjusted spread (OAS). A portfolio of such loans is equivalent to a mortgage backed security (MBS) and, hence, the OAS can be estimated from the pricing of the federally insured MBSs issued by Ginnie Mae that are backed by FHA-insured mortgages.

Specifically, holders of MBSs receive the scheduled principal and interest of the underlying mortgages (net of fees associated with administering the loan) while the mortgages are active, but the holders' principal is returned in full for mortgages that default or prepay; although investors in MBSs are insured against default on the underlying mortgages, they are still exposed to the risk from changes in the rates of prepayment, for which they demand a spread (the OAS) over Treasury securities of comparable maturity. To estimate that spread for a representative set of FHA mortgages, CBO simulates the cash flows that an MBS investor would receive using the statistical default and prepayment model and solves for the spread over the Treasury rates in those simulations that equate the present value of the cash flows to the market price of the security. CBO estimates an average spread to be roughly 70 basis points in 2014.

Valuing Nonguaranteed Loans. To determine the value of a nonguaranteed loan, the cash flows associated with that loan are discounted at the Treasury note rate plus the sum of the OAS and the market risk premium that investors would require to hold such a loan. Investors holding a portfolio of such loans would bear credit risk in addition to the prepayment risk of an MBS. Thus, the market risk premium compensates investors for the risk of default losses. That premium is the most important driver of the difference between the FCRA and fair-value subsidy rates.

However, the market risk premium cannot be observed directly and therefore must be estimated. CBO estimates the premium for a representative portfolio of FHA mortgages using two different approaches as well as consultation with outside experts. (The Appendix discusses the sensitivity of the results to the estimated premium.) One approach is to estimate the risk premium for FHA's 100 percent insurance coverage from the partial insurance coverage provided by private mortgage insurers. Variation in the private insurers' pricing schedules across different coverage levels provides a way to extrapolate how much more the private mortgage insurers would charge to cover all losses on a given mortgage. The difference between that extrapolated fee and an estimate of the expected losses plus the insurer's annualized administrative costs for that loan gives an estimate of the risk premium.

The other approach is to combine the fees for partial coverage set by private insurers with the fees set by Fannie Mae and Freddie Mac, which take the residual risk on the privately insured mortgages that they purchase. One complication with that approach is that, because of the GSEs' federal backing, CBO estimates that the GSEs charge lower fees than a fully private insurer would. Thus, using the GSEs' fees understates the true risk premium and requires an additional adjustment.

In those approaches to estimating the risk premium, CBO does not subtract an estimate of the taxes that insurers would need to pay from the prices that they charge, and so the estimates implicitly include a tax charge. Including that tax charge in the fair-value estimate for FHA's insurance recognizes the opportunity cost of the tax revenues the federal government foregoes when it, not private insurers, insures mortgages. If such estimates were to be used in the federal budget or for official CBO cost estimates, care would need to be taken to avoid counting twice the effects of those taxes.

Using those approaches, CBO estimates that the market risk premium is 115 basis points in 2014. The two approaches gave similar estimates of the risk premium, and were consistent with the opinions of outside experts.

Valuing FHA's Fees. The cash flows associated with FHA's fees are discounted at the same rate as the cash flows associated with the nonguaranteed loan because those fees are also subject to default risk.

Estimated Subsidy Rates. To compute the present values of the simulated cash flows associated with FHA's mortgage guarantees, CBO discounts the cash flows using Treasury interest rates plus the relevant risk premiums. The Treasury rates vary stochastically across the simulations described in section 6.2. As a result, cash flows are discounted more heavily in simulation paths with high interest rates than in paths with low interest rates. Because fair-value estimates are forward-looking measures, only cash flows that had not been realized by the end of fiscal year 2013 are included in the fair-value estimates, and the cash flows are discounted to that date. To facilitate comparison between the fair-value and FCRA estimates, CBO also estimated the net present value of those cash flows as of the end of fiscal year 2013 using FCRA discount rates.

Table 7.4 shows CBO's estimates of the fair-value subsidy rates and costs of FHA's 1992 through 2015 cohorts. Because the analysis includes only cash flows after the end of fiscal year 2013, it omits the up-front and annual premiums paid for the cohorts prior to 2014. The inclusion of the up-front premium for the 2014 and 2015 cohorts accounts for much of the decrease in their estimated fair-value subsidy rates relative to the 2013 to 2014 cohorts.

Table 7.4 also displays CBO's estimates of the FCRA subsidy rates of those cohorts including only cash flows after the end of fiscal year 2013. For the 2014 and 2015 cohorts, the reported rates are equal to the lifetime FCRA subsidy rates reported in Table 7.1; for the earlier cohorts, the reported rates are larger (less negative or more positive) than the lifetime subsidy rates in Table 7.1, because of the omission of the cash flows that occurred before fiscal 2014, such as the up-front premiums. The FCRA-based subsidy rates are lower than the estimated fair-value subsidy rates, reflecting the cost of the market risk associated with the loan guarantees.

The combined estimated FCRA subsidy rate for the 2014 and 2015 cohorts is negative 5.5 percent, while the estimated fair-value subsidy rate is positive 0.7 percent. Therefore, accounting for the market risk associated with those loan guarantees eliminates the estimated cost savings for those cohorts.

Table 7.5 presents projected fair-value subsidy rates for purchase loans in the 2014 cohort categorized by loan-to-value ratio and borrower FICO score. The table breaks the subsidy rate (panel C) into its components of fee income (panel A) and guarantee value (panel B).

Loans with an original loan-to-value ratio of 90 percent or lower are eligible for cancellation of annual fees at 11 years of age, while other loans pay the annual fee to maturity. As a result, loans with higher original loan-to-value ratios tend to pay annual fees for a longer period than lower LTV loans, making the present value of fee income generally greater for loans with higher original LTVs. Loans with lower borrower credit scores and higher LTV ratios are at higher risk of default, and therefore generally have higher values of the guarantee.

Because FHA's fees do not vary according to borrower FICO score but the value of the guarantee does, there is a pattern of cross-subsidies among FHA borrowers. Loan categories with borrower credit scores greater than 680 and LTV ratios greater than 95 have negative estimated fair-value subsidy rates because those relatively high credit scores predict low claim rates and those relatively high LTV ratios predict high fee income. Other loan categories have positive estimated fair-value subsidy rates because they have higher predicted claim rates or lower predicted fee income.

Cohort	Unpaid Principal Balance ($ Billions)	FCRA-Based Subsidy Rate[1]	Fair-Value Subsidy Rate[1]	Fair-Value Subsidy Cost ($ Billions)[1]
Table 7.4: Projected FCRA and Fair-Value Subsidy Rates for Outstanding Loans				
1992	0.7	-0.3%	5.7%	0.0
1993	1.3	-0.7%	6.9%	0.1
1994	1.9	-0.7%	6.7%	0.1
1995	0.9	0.2%	6.0%	0.1
1996	1.5	0.6%	7.7%	0.1
1997	1.7	1.1%	7.5%	0.1
1998	3.1	0.9%	6.7%	0.2
1999	4.9	1.0%	5.9%	0.3
2000	2.7	2.7%	6.2%	0.2
2001	5.0	4.9%	9.1%	0.5
2002	8.7	5.9%	10.7%	0.9
2003	22.4	5.5%	9.3%	2.1
2004	19.0	9.8%	15.5%	2.9
2005	18.1	10.3%	14.8%	2.7
2006	16.2	10.3%	14.8%	2.4
2007	19.4	8.1%	11.6%	2.3
2008	57.4	7.1%	12.1%	7.0
2009	148.8	3.3%	8.1%	12.1
2010	187.3	2.4%	5.4%	10.2
2011	148.0	-0.2%	3.1%	4.6
2012	184.9	-1.6%	3.2%	6.0
2013	233.6	-2.4%	3.7%	8.6
Subtotal: Historical Cohorts	1087.6	1.3%	5.8%	63.4
2014	150.0	-5.7%	0.7%	1.0
2015	149.7	-5.3%	0.7%	1.0
Subtotal: Future Cohorts	299.7	-5.5%	0.7%	2.0
Total	1387.3	-0.2%	4.7%	65.4

Notes:

1. The reported subsidy rates consider only cash flows projected to occur in fiscal year 2014 and afterwards, not cash flows over the entire life of the cohort. The FCRA-based subsidy rates reflect the present value of future cash flows discounted at Treasury rates of interest, while the fair-value rates reflect the present value of future cash flows discounted at approximate market rates of interest. The future cash flows for the historical cohorts were discounted to the end of fiscal year 2013 under both methods. Those present values are divided by the outstanding principal balance from each cohort to calculate the reported subsidy rate.

Table 7.5: Projected Fair-Value Subsidy Rates by Loan Characteristics, 2014 Cohort (Purchase Loans Only)

Panel A: Value of Fee Income

	Borrower FICO Score[1]						
LTV Ratio[2]	500 to 559	560 to 599	600 to 639	640 to 659	660 to 679	680 to 719	≥ 720
<80	5.6%	5.1%	5.0%	4.9%	4.9%	4.9%	5.2%
80 to 90	5.8%	5.6%	5.5%	5.4%	5.5%	5.5%	5.6%
90 to 95	8.5%	7.3%	6.0%	6.0%	6.1%	6.0%	6.5%
95 to 97		8.9%	8.9%	8.9%	8.9%	8.4%	8.6%
≥ 97		8.4%	8.3%	8.2%	8.2%	7.8%	7.9%

Panel B: Value of Guarantee

	Borrower FICO Score						
LTV Ratio	500 to 559	560 to 599	600 to 639	640 to 659	660 to 679	680 to 719	≥ 720
<80	9.4%	7.4%	7.0%	6.0%	6.1%	5.7%	5.5%
80 to 90	11.6%	10.0%	9.2%	7.8%	8.0%	7.3%	6.4%
90 to 95	11.4%	10.8%	9.9%	8.2%	8.5%	7.6%	6.9%
95 to 97		11.5%	11.1%	9.1%	9.4%	7.9%	7.2%
≥ 97		11.5%	11.1%	8.7%	8.9%	7.5%	6.7%

Panel C: Subsidy Rate[3]

	Borrower FICO Score						
LTV Ratio	500 to 559	560 to 599	600 to 639	640 to 659	660 to 679	680 to 719	≥ 720
<80	3.9%	2.3%	2.0%	1.2%	1.2%	0.8%	0.3%
80 to 90	5.8%	4.4%	3.7%	2.4%	2.5%	1.8%	0.8%
90 to 95	2.9%	3.5%	3.9%	2.1%	2.4%	1.5%	0.4%
95 to 97		2.7%	2.2%	0.2%	0.5%	-0.4%	-1.4%
≥ 97		3.1%	2.8%	0.5%	0.7%	-0.3%	-1.2%

Notes:

1. Borrower FICO score is the borrower's credit score as reported by FHA.

2. LTV Ratio is the ratio of the original mortgage amount to the value of the mortgaged property at the time of loan origination.

3. Subsidy Rate equals value of fee income minus value of guarantee.

Loan categories with negative subsidy rates would produce cost savings for taxpayers, according to CBO's analysis, even when evaluated at private market discount rates. Those savings imply that private investors in an orderly market could guarantee such loans profitably under FHA's 2014 fee schedule. If FHA's fees remain unchanged, its market share in loan categories with an estimated negative subsidy rate on a fair-value basis may decline in the future as borrowers find alternative sources of mortgage financing.

7.3 Issues with Accounting for Refinances of Previously FHA-insured Mortgages

CBO's FCRA and fair-value subsidy calculations treat refinances of previously FHA-insured mortgages, such as streamline refinances, as new originations in the cohort in which the refinancing occurs, consistent with the subsidies reported in the federal budget. Aragon and others (2010) and Caplin and others (2012) argue that treating those refinances as new originations misattributes the risk that a borrower poses to FHA across cohorts. They argue that the costs associated with those loans should instead be linked to the cohort in which the original loans were guaranteed. In particular, because borrowers acquire the option to streamline refinance when they take out the original loan, FHA accepts the risk posed by streamline refinances when the original loans are guaranteed. One rationale for treating refinances as new loans for budgetary purposes is that FHA's programs are discretionary, meaning that their activity must be authorized by annual appropriations bills. Therefore, the current budgetary treatment attributes costs to the cohort under which the refinances were authorized. (In contrast, for student loans, which do not require annual appropriations bills, CBO treats consolidation loans as extensions of the original loans rather than as new loans.[17])

Aragon and others (2010) and Caplin and others (2012) also argue that failing to track refinance loans across cohorts could lead to underestimated costs. Streamline refinances are likely to compose a higher proportion of FHA's new guarantees when the housing market is distressed and FHA borrowers face more difficulty refinancing into non-FHA loans. The model does not account for that state dependence in simulating FHA's new cohorts. Therefore, the model may understate total expected default costs and, hence, the FCRA and fair-value subsidies.

Furthermore, risk premiums are likely to be elevated when streamline refinances are more numerous. That correlation between risk premiums and the number of streamline refinances would lead the weighted-average fair-value subsidy across the possible simulation paths to exceed the fair-value subsidy evaluated at the average risk premium and average streamline refinance volume. Thus, accounting for that correlation would increase the estimated average fair-value subsidy associated with those loans compared to the current approach. However, that effect may be counteracted to some extent by the reduction in defaults arising from the lower interest rates and stronger credit profiles that the average FHA borrowers are likely to have in a weak economy.

Overall, CBO estimates that any understatement of FCRA and fair-value subsidies owing to those effects is unlikely to be large, but those effects may widen the distribution of potential costs relative to the distribution generated by the model simulations.

---

[17] See, for example, Congressional Budget Office (2010) or Lucas and Moore (2007).

Appendix

CBO's simulation model is meant to reflect several sources of uncertainty, including uncertainty about future macroeconomic and housing market conditions, uncertainty about the statistical model's parameters, and uncertainty regarding actual default and prepayment behavior probabilities relative to the predictions of the statistical model. However, the simulations do not account for other sources of uncertainty that could affect the performance of FHA's portfolio, such as changes in FHA policy, the broader housing and mortgage markets, or the characteristics of FHA's future loan guarantees. The simulations also do not account for the possibility that future economic conditions may exhibit more or less variation than CBO has estimated based on historical data. In order to assess the sensitivity of the results to some of those factors, the appendix examines several other sources of uncertainty related to the characteristics of future cohorts, the effects of FHA's recent loss mitigation strategies, and the size of the market risk premium. Although it is not feasible for CBO to analyze every potential source of uncertainty regarding the budgetary costs of FHA's single-family mortgage insurance, the sources of uncertainty reflected in the main analysis and in the Appendix represent the main sources of uncertainty that are likely to have a significant impact on the estimates in CBO's judgment.

Table A.1 presents the projected lifetime claim, prepayment, and loss given default rates for the 1992 to 2015 cohorts. The table contains the average across all model simulations as well as the 5th and 95th percentiles across simulations. The numbers in the table correspond to the averages and percentiles displayed in Figure 6.4. Those percentiles reflect the uncertainty arising from the sources considered in the main analysis but not the uncertainty arising from the additional sources considered in the Appendix.

CBO considered four alternative scenarios to explore the sensitivity of the simulation outcomes for the 2014 and 2015 cohorts to key modeling parameters. The scenarios include lower average borrower FICO scores, higher loan-to-value ratios for streamline refinances, lower loss given default, and lower market risk premiums, respectively. Table A.2 presents the results for each of the scenarios.

The first scenario examines the effect of lower borrower FICO scores than CBO uses in the main analysis, which is an average score of just over 690 for both the 2014 and 2015 cohorts. The alternative scenario, labeled "Lower FICO Scores," uses an average borrower FICO score of 681 for the 2014 cohort and 675 for the 2015 cohort. Those average FICO scores would represent a swifter return to historical averages than in the main analysis. The lifetime claim rates for both cohorts rise in the scenario relative to the main analysis while the lifetime prepayment rates fall. The credit subsidy rates for both cohorts rise slightly using both FCRA and fair-value estimates.

FHA's streamline refinance program does not require a new house price appraisal, so estimating the LTVs of those loans is difficult. In CBO's main analysis, streamline refinances are projected to have the same distribution of LTVs as nonstreamline refinances. CBO performed tests of its model to assess the reasonableness of its assumption in light of the concerns raised by Aragon and others (2010) and Caplin and others (2012) that streamline refinances are likely to have higher LTVs than nonstreamline refinances. In those tests, CBO compared the claim and prepayment rates that the model predicts for streamline refinances in its base case over the historical period for which CBO has data. Those model predictions are out of sample in the sense that streamline refinances were generally excluded from the main analysis because their loan records lacked necessary data, but they are in-sample in the sense that

	Table A.1: Projected Lifetime Claim and Prepayment Rate Distributions								
	Claims			Prepayments			Loss Given Default		
Cohort	Average	5th Percentile	95th Percentile	Average	5th Percentile	95th Percentile	Average	5th Percentile	95th Percentile
1992	7.1	7.0	7.2	90.4	89.5	91.1	48.7	48.5	49.0
1993	6.5	6.3	6.6	90.4	89.3	91.3	45.1	44.7	45.5
1994	7.2	7.0	7.3	89.5	88.3	90.6	42.3	41.7	42.8
1995	9.8	9.6	10.0	88.3	87.3	89.1	44.9	44.6	45.4
1996	8.7	8.5	8.9	89.0	88.0	89.9	45.4	44.8	46.0
1997	8.2	8.0	8.4	89.9	89.0	90.6	45.5	44.9	46.2
1998	7.1	7.0	7.4	90.7	89.7	91.5	45.3	44.5	46.1
1999	7.7	7.5	8.0	90.2	89.2	91.0	46.9	46.0	48.0
2000	8.7	8.4	9.0	90.5	89.9	90.9	51.3	50.5	52.3
2001	8.3	7.9	8.8	90.3	89.5	91.1	54.4	52.9	56.2
2002	9.0	8.3	9.8	88.6	87.3	89.6	57.9	55.4	61.1
2003	14.6	12.9	16.5	79.7	76.5	82.5	57.5	52.8	63.1
2004	19.0	16.5	21.8	74.0	69.8	77.5	58.8	53.2	65.7
2005	28.2	23.9	32.9	62.2	54.9	68.6	62.1	55.7	69.8
2006	29.2	24.2	35.1	61.2	54.2	67.4	62.8	56.8	70.0
2007	30.2	24.8	36.0	61.8	55.3	68.0	59.7	54.4	66.1
2008	20.6	15.9	26.0	68.7	62.5	74.3	56.4	49.5	64.9
2009	12.6	9.0	16.8	75.4	68.3	80.5	49.7	40.4	61.1
2010	10.3	7.0	14.5	83.8	75.9	89.5	46.9	35.0	61.4
2011	5.2	3.1	8.3	90.8	83.1	95.5	41.5	27.2	58.8
2012	4.7	2.1	9.2	87.8	76.8	94.9	49.0	32.6	69.5
2013	6.7	2.3	14.4	83.9	68.3	94.2	50.2	33.7	71.0
2014	7.6	2.6	15.9	85.1	70.0	95.5	47.9	31.5	68.8
2015	8.3	2.7	16.7	85.7	69.8	96.3	46.9	30.5	67.8

Note: Projected lifetime claim, prepayment, and loss given default rates are calculated assuming streamline refinances have approximately the same default, prepayment and loss given default experience as nonstreamline refinances in the same cohorts. (See section 6.1 for more details.)

the relevant macroeconomic and housing market conditions are already known and were used to estimate the model. The model predicted claim rates for the streamline refinances that were substantially higher than what was actually observed in the data for the cohorts from 1992 through 2000, and it predicted claim rates that were close to, although generally still higher than, those observed in the actual data for the 2001 to 2010 cohorts. For the 2011 to 2013 cohorts, the model slightly underpredicted the observed cumulative claim rates for streamline refinances. At the same time, the model overpredicted cumulative prepayment rates for those cohorts, which will tend to counteract the effect of underestimating claim rates on the estimated subsidy rates for those cohorts.

To assess the sensitivity of the model results to the extent of negative equity, the second scenario examines the effects of higher LTVs for FHA's streamline refinances. In the scenario, the streamline

Cohort	Main Analysis	Lower FICO Scores	Higher SLR LTVs	Lower Loss Given Default	Lower Market Risk Premium
2014:					
Lifetime Claim Rate	7.6%	8.1%	10.5%	7.6%	7.6%
Lifetime Prepayment Rate	85.1%	84.6%	81.9%	85.1%	85.1%
FCRA Subsidy Rate	-5.65%	-5.41%	-4.68%	-6.40%	-5.65%
Fair-value Subsidy Rate	0.70%	0.86%	1.64%	0.03%	-0.58%
2015:					
Lifetime Claim Rate	8.3%	9.4%	10.6%	8.3%	8.3%
Lifetime Prepayment Rate	85.7%	84.2%	83.3%	85.7%	85.7%
FCRA Subsidy Rate	-5.32%	-5.11%	-4.56%	-6.12%	-5.32%
Fair-value Subsidy Rate	0.70%	0.96%	1.42%	-0.02%	-0.53%

Table A.2: Sensitivity of Projections to Alternative Assumptions

refinances in the 2014 and 2015 cohorts have an average loan-to-value ratio approximately 30 percentage points higher than the average in the main analysis. CBO recently acquired data from FHA that suggests that streamline refinances are unlikely to have average loan-to-value ratios much higher than in the main analysis, thus making the scenario an extreme case. However, the scenario does give a sense of how sensitive the estimated subsidy rates are to the loan-to-value ratios of the streamline refinances. The lifetime claim rates for the 2014 and 2015 cohorts are about 3 and 2.3 percentage points higher, respectively, than in the main analysis because streamline refinances are projected to make up a smaller proportion of loans in the 2015 cohort. The estimated FCRA subsidy rate rises nearly one percentage point for the 2014 cohort and about 0.8 percentage points for the 2015 cohort. The distribution of the FCRA subsidy rates is also wider in the second scenario than in the main analysis because the performance of higher-LTV loans is more sensitive to house price movements. The spread between the 5th and 95th percentiles of the subsidy rate for the 2014 cohort rises half a percentage point from the base case to the second scenario.

The third scenario examines the effects of lower loss given default. The scenario could be pertinent if FHA's programs for loss mitigation, such as increased use of pre-foreclosure sales, third-party sales, and note sales result in lower losses given default than CBO projects in the main analysis. The projected lifetime claim and prepayment rates do not to change in the scenario, but the average loss given default is expected to be 30 percent lower. The FCRA subsidy rate falls about 75 basis points for the 2014 cohort and about 80 basis points for the 2015 cohort in the scenario.

The fourth scenario examines the effects of a lower market risk premium; specifically, 90 basis points in both 2014 and 2015, or 25 basis points lower than in the main analysis. The estimated claim and prepayment rates, as well as the estimated FCRA subsidy rates, do not change. However, the reduction in the market risk premium results in lower estimated fair-value subsidy rates. The estimated fair-value subsidy rate falls approximately 125 basis points for both cohorts.

References

Ambrose, Brent, Charles Capone, and Yongheng Deng, "Optimal Put Exercise: An Empirical Examination of Conditions for Mortgage Foreclosure," *Journal of Real Estate Finance and Economics,* vol. 23, no. 2 (September 2001), pp. 213–234, http://dx.doi.org/10.1023/A:1011110501074.

Aragon, Diego, Andrew Caplin, Umit Chopra, John V. Leahy, Marco Scoffier, and Joseph Tracy, *Reassessing FHA Risk,* Working Paper 15802 (National Bureau of Economic Research, March 2010), www.nber.org/papers/w15802.pdf.

Bajari, Patrick, Chenghuan Sean Chu, and Minjung Park, *An Empirical Model of Subprime Mortgage Default from 2000 to 2007,* Working Paper 14625 (National Bureau of Economic Research, December 2008), www.nber.org/papers/w14625.

Bhutta, Neil, Jane Dokko, and Hui Shan, *The Depth of Negative Equity and Mortgage Default Decisions,* Finance and Economics Discussion Series Paper 2010-35 (Board of Governors of the Federal Reserve System, May 2010), www.federalreserve.gov/pubs/feds/2010/201035.

Brealey, Richard, Stewart Myers, and Franklin Allen, *Principles of Corporate Finance*, 8th ed. (McGraw-Hill/Irwin, 2006), Ch. 24.

Caplin, Andrew, Anna Cororaton, and Joseph Tracy, *Is the FHA Creating Sustainable Homeownership?* Working Paper 18190 (National Bureau of Economic Research, June 2012), www.nber.org/papers/w18190.pdf.

Clapp, John, Gerson Goldberg, John Harding, and Michael LaCour-Little, "Movers and Shuckers: Interdependent Prepayment Decisions," *Real Estate Economics,* vol. 29, no. 3 (December 2002), pp. 411–450, http://dx.doi.org/10.1111/1080-8620.00017.

Clapp, John, Yongheng Deng, and Xudong An, "Unobserved Heterogeneity in Models of Competing Mortgage Termination Risks," *Real Estate Economics*, vol. 34, no. 2 (June 2006), pp. 243–273, http://dx.doi.org/10.2139/ssrn.512624.

Congressional Budget Office, *Costs and Policy Options for Federal Student Loan Programs* (March 2010), www.cbo.gov/publication/21018.

Congressional Budget Office, *Fair-Value Accounting for Federal Credit Programs* (March 2012), www.cbo.gov/publication/43027.

Congressional Budget Office, *The 2013 Long-Term Budget Outlook* (September 2013a), www.cbo.gov/publication/44521.

Congressional Budget Office, "How FHA's Mutual Mortgage Insurance Fund Accounts for the Cost of Mortgage Guarantees," *CBO Blog,* (October 22, 2013b), www.cbo.gov/publication/44634.

Congressional Budget Office, *The Budget and Economic Outlook: 2014 to 2024* (February 2014), www.cbo.gov/publication/45010.

Congressional Budget Office, Testimony of Douglas W. Elmendorf before the Committee on Financial Services, U.S. House of Representatives, *Estimates of the Cost of Credit Programs of the Export-Import Bank* (June 25, 2014), www.cbo.gov/publication/45468.

Deng, Yongheng, John Quigley, and Robert van Order, "Mortgage Terminations, Heterogeneity and the Exercise of Mortgage Options," *Econometrica*, vol. 68, no. 2 (March 2000), pp. 275–307, http://dx.doi.org/10.1111/1468-0262.00110.

Department of Housing and Urban Development, *Actuarial Review of the Federal Housing Administration Mutual Mortgage Insurance Fund, Forward Loans, for Fiscal Year 2013* (prepared by Integrated Financial Engineering, Inc., December 2013a), http://go.usa.gov/8fke.

Department of Housing and Urban Development, *Actuarial Review of FHA's Mutual Mortgage Insurance Fund for Forward Loans (Excluding HECM)* (prepared by Summit Consulting, LLC, and Milliman, Inc., December 2013b), http://go.usa.gov/8f8V.

Department of Housing and Urban Development, *FHA Single Family Mutual Mortgage Insurance Fund Programs: Quarterly Report to Congress* (various years), http://go.usa.gov/8wMW.

Elul, Ronel, Nicholas Souleles, Souphala Chomsisengphet, Dennis Glennon, and Robert Hunt, "What 'Triggers' Mortgage Default?" *American Economic Review: Papers and Proceedings,* vol. 100, no. 2 (May 2010), pp. 490–494, http://dx.doi.org/10.1257/aer.100.2.490.

Foote, Christopher, Kristopher Gerardi, Lorenz Goette, and Paul Willen, "Reducing Foreclosures: No Easy Answers," *NBER Macroeconomics Annual 2009,* vol. 24 (April 2010), pp. 89–138, www.nber.org/chapters/c11790.

Government Accountability Office, *FHA Mortgage Insurance: Applicability of Industry Requirements is Limited, but Certain Features Could Enhance Oversight*, GAO-13-722 (September 2013), www.gao.gov/assets/660/657511.pdf.

Guiso, Luigi, Paola Sapienza, and Luigi Zingales, "The Determinants of Attitudes Towards Strategic Default on Mortgages," *Journal of Finance*, vol. 68, no. 4 (August 2013), pp. 1473–1515, http://dx.doi.org/10.1111/jofi.12044.

Gyourko, Joseph, and Joseph Tracy, "Reconciling Theory and Empirics on the Role of Unemployment in Mortgage Default," *Journal of Urban Economics*, vol. 80 (March 2014), pp. 87–96, http://dx.doi.org/10.1016/j.jue.2013.10.005.

Kau, James and Donald Keenan, "An Overview of the Option-Theoretic Pricing of Mortgages," *Journal of Housing Research*, vol. 6, no. 2 (1995), pp. 217–244, http://tinyurl.com/kt7cmrt.

Lucas, Deborah and Damien Moore, "The Student Loan Consolidation Option: An Analysis of an Exotic Financial Derivative," CBO Working Paper 2007-05, www.cbo.gov/publication/18540.

Mortgage Bankers Association, *National Delinquency Survey Results Q3 2013* (Mortgage Bankers Association, 2013).

Pence, Karen, "Foreclosing on Opportunity: State Laws and Mortgage Credit," *Review of Economics and Statistics*, vol. 88, no. 1 (February 2006), pp. 177–182, http://dx.doi.org/10.1162/rest.2006.88.1.177.

Pennington-Cross, Anthony and Joseph Nichols, "Credit History and the FHA-Conventional Choice," *Real Estate Economics*, vol. 28, no. 2 (2000), pp.307–336, http://dx.doi.org/10.1111/1540-6229.00803.

Qi, Min and Xiaolong Yang, "Loss Given Default of High Loan-to-Value Residential Mortgages," *Journal of Banking and Finance*, vol. 33, no. 5 (May 2009), pp. 788–799, http://dx.doi.org/10.1016/j.jbankfin.2008.09.010.

Qi, Min and Xinlei Zhao, "Comparison of Modeling Methods for Loss Given Default," *Journal of Banking and Finance*, vol. 35, no. 11 (November 2011), pp. 2842–2855, http://dx.doi.org/10.1016/j.jbankfin.2011.03.011.